LIVING WITH WOMEN AND THE WORLD AROUND US

JOHN PEERY

Living With Women and the World Around Us
Published by Heavy Lenses Press
Littleton, CO

ISBN: 979-8-9878845-0-8
POETRY / American / General

Cover and interior design by Victoria Wolf, wolfdesignandmarketing.com, copyright owned by John Peery

Printed in the United States of America.

johnpeeryauthor.com

For those I love
And have loved
And those that love
And have loved me

CONTENTS

THURSDAY

WEDNESDAY

TUESDAY

MONDAY

SUNDAY

SATURDAY

MISTS AND FOG

Mists and fogs, striations of color and intensity
lie impenetrable across the future,
Veiling all paths and options,
obscuring design, purpose and pattern.
Cloudy wastes of willowing winds chastise the desire
To stay immediate,
to stay focused on that which cannot be seen.
There are no signposts apparent,
no orientation given
Save the internal compass that has weathered with time.
That which was important,
A focused commitment to succeed, to triumph,
driving a life forward, has withered,
Replaced by a vacuum of intent and purpose.

What is it that now anoints a new age,
a new passion for action?
Not filling the hours with frittered affairs unfulfilling.
He cooks food for himself sparingly,
invites friends less frequently,
Sharing meals and conversation superficially, taking little satisfaction.

A path may become apparent,
may clear amidst the cloudy firmament,
may originate from the introspective work,
the chasing down of past ghosts, lost haunts.
New figments of insight may arise from opaque remembrances while
Tops of trees and tips of temples punctuate the swirling mass of gray
Inspiring visions of oases ahead, yet
Deceiving distances and direction in the tentative light
Provide no starting point or end,
no lighthouse of knowledge,
No yellow brick road through the malaise.

He stands. Feet firmly planted on the edge of tomorrow,
On the edge of the X that marks "You are here."
He knows where he is, knows who he is,
but where is he going, or should?
As seasons change, the enclosing mists remain
Fog cuddling tightly round him.
A misty overlay of concern and disquiet
creates a tempo of movement that is languid,
Movement without the intent of purpose.
Purposeless without direction,
Slowing the knowing footsteps that could create a future.

The sun bravely tries to negotiate passage through the cloud deck,
Attempts to burn away the mists and fogs,
but is dispatched without honor.
He is suspicious of the step into nothingness,
Not knowing what the outcome might be,
Without recognition of the possibilities,
the simmering cauldron of uncertainty,
Loath to take that first big step north or south, east or west
No understanding of how to step and when
without some vision of what will come
In the waning of his days,
undetermined by length or quality.

He waits, itching to move both right and left, forward and back
And that inclination prevents movement.
He is aware of everything,
and nothing,
remembers all, and forgets easily,
Taking clues from the poems he writes,
the letters he never completes,
The stories and dreams seething in his psyche,
pushing through his reticence.

Thoughts splashing onto paper bring relief but no guidance.
He writes alone in the quiet chamber of his room,
surrounded by his art,
Enveloped by the paintings and sculpture,
the books and treasures,
alone
In the embryonic stage of decision,
the zygote of creation that could lead to a path
That will direct him through the smoggy fog dispatching sight.

He will see, he believes,
will feel that direction through the soles of his shoes,
Will proceed to discover that which is unknown,
will find a compass remade,
A directional of self,
a concreteness of purpose,
a revolution of intent.
This will happen, he feels it.
He reminds himself of this truth frequently and fervently

Yet he knows that he is old,
The calendar does not lie, cannot extend his time
He wonders if his efforts will be rewarded,.
Wonders if his days are too numbered,
Constrained by the body's revolt, the arthritis and disrepair
Developed in the thoughtless progression of life
Will there be a next life to live in extension
Before his cells bid good bye,
Before the neural reaches of authenticity decay
He forges ahead with his quest expecting the best.
Another goal to achieve in a life of achievement,
Another hurrah for the soul.

THE TREE IN AUTUMN

My monstrous tree across the way
The tree that controls them all it seems
The harbinger of seasons
Has shown signs of Autumn
Sparkling in the last light of the day.
A bit there, up high, a branch golden
Reflecting the sun's last efforts
A bit lower, patches of promise
A tantalizing preview of what is to come.
The tree teases the senses
Suggests what might be in the coming days
A glorious explosion of color
A celebration of the past season
That provided shade and cool repose
For all that sought shelter
From the summer's heat.
The tree heralds the change of seasons
It will be time for rest, a respite,

From the awesome burden it
Accepted in the spring and fulfilled so well.
Rest well my friend
I look forward to your rebirth
Your renewed promise for the future
I will enjoy your leafless skeleton
Over the winter's chill, your branches
Frosted, snow piled inches deep
Until once more I view green
And once more
As you have done for generations
You take up your mantle
And provide what is needed.

SPIRITS

The spirits were scheming within him
Plotting facial tics and palsied steps
Jealous and angered by his denial of their existence
Intent on proving that he could not ignore
their sway,
their control of his future.

He,
supposed master of his domain,
Conductor of his rhythms, his focused self
Denied their control, ignored their intent
planned his growth like a garden
Fertilizing his imagination,
sowing his disregard.

The struggle eternal between that which has come before
And that which is still to come
Plays awkwardly in stolen moments
Silent stills protected in albums black and white
Colored recollections of that which was and is.

The spirits move in determined paths,
Perhaps predetermined paths untrod
Negating the decisions made,
the choices
Cataloging the chances taken in unthinking moments
Taking advantage of age and inexperience.

Spirits squeeze the now with ancestral remembrance
Genetic forewarnings of limited existence.
Sketch the fathers and mothers existential
Give fair warning of their intended mastery
Their predilection to direct their chartered territory.

He,
noting the coming genesis of awareness,
Aware of that which is and was in the dawning of his genes
Aware of the subtle turn of the earth beneath his heels
Aware of the intrusive ritual of obedience to the spirits
Rebels,
throws his days into the cauldron
Into the unmeasured creation of the future.

He will not be held captive by the past
Will not succumb to the numbing expectations of lives
Throws open the door to eternity
Realizes that the future is his to decide
His to determine in the cosmic charade of circumstances.
He charges wide eyed into the future.

GATHERED

They are all here
All of my lovers from the past
Grouped together grinning, in various stages of dress and undress
They haven't changed a bit,
Christine still 17 with a pert come-hither smile
Janet who loved me madly one night into morning
Jeanne still seems ready for bed and
Ann spared from her decline looking fit
And the others, not so many as to crowd the room
But enough for a lifetime
I get up to go to the bathroom
They are standing in line
From the bedroom to the bathroom
Watching my naked body,
That once was and is no longer.
Their eyes sparkle with enjoyment
I pretend not to notice them, ignore their smiles
Preferring to go about my business
Then return to bed and sleep.
I am confident they will be gone in the morning
They only arrive in the darkness
They do not intrude or comment but they witness
The aging body, the sun damaged skull, the loss of hair.
They are welcome, I suppose
They are my past.
They are a part of the me that grew through time

Most added something, sometimes huge
Some took more than they gave.
I smile, pull the sheets into a shell around my head
And prepare to go to sleep.
Good night ladies. I am sure I will see you again.
Best wishes to you all.

DEAD TREE

That tree is dead
Shining in its nakedness
Bark stripped from limb and trunk
Polished by winds and rain, silver gray
Etched against the forest's flora, deepest green
It is a skeletal remembrance of its past
Yet stark in its statement of performance
A sliver of what was once
A naked precursor of the future
Proud and upright in the completion of its life
A signpost of the future, in raving contrast.
The bare bones of the tree provide context
To the struggle to be present, to be alert,
To be aware of the future and to move with resolution
Engaging that which comes.
We will all die, disappear, leave nothing but the refuse
Or will we leave an impression, a statement that we lived,
An ongoing plunge into the past as it is present.
Will your skeleton grace the future in extended licensure
To provide depth to the photo
Relief to the young striving?
The dead tree stands alert, a reminder of the past,
A signpost for the future.

SHEDDING STUFF

I have moved from my house
shedding years of lives
50 years of days,
accumulations of this and that
Much given to those who might like what I have had.
My hope is that they will use those possessions
For years to come.
I work to release my connection
to things unrelated to my present life.
I am alone and the detritus of my past life must go.
I buy a new bed, new sheets, new pillows a comforter that has color.
I move into a new life of unexpected dimensions,
a new milieu of substance.
What will I take from the past into the future?
What will be retained?
There are scars that I have learned to live with
Physical and emotional that are stuck to my body and psyche.
They will stay.
There are memories of happy times and successes that shall be kept.
The rest, the stuff, will go,
replaced by new stuff which is mine

QUIET

It is so quiet
A random cricket rubbing its legs together
The only disturbance in the afternoon
There is no breeze, air still
No leaves moving, stasis
A silent cloak of civility in repose
The sun slides quietly over the horizon
The blue deepens insinuating
A change to black
Sitting on my balcony in the late
Evening's collection of skies
Clear of storm and strife
Undisturbed and calm
Brings thoughts of you.
I wish you were here to disturb the night
To disturb me alone with my thoughts
Alone with the air barely breathing
Alone in longing for connection
Where are you when I need you most?

JUICY FRUIT BUBBLES

They lived together forever
Among the bagatelles
Blowing juicy fruit bubbles
Scratching the sand from behind their ears

Porcelain pals cluttered the shelves in clusters
Shiny cliques of glass and ceramic
Barely dusted by life and neglect
Feather boas attached to canes

Among the corduroy divans
Atop the hardwood floors
Trays of divinity, crystal cups with tea
Prattle about the weather

They lived together forever amidst the chintz and lace
An occasional Agatha Christie
Amongst the Lewis Carroll,
The ardent vocals of Edith Piaf.

Smoke rings and rings of port filled glasses
Dominoes atop the Times
A maze of numbers and words
With the crossword done in ink

Beneath the shake shingles
Inside the ivied walls
Their pattern of existence was created
From the puttering attention to the mundane

They lived forever together
Bonds of gold and flesh
Their hearts stitched together by time
Their lives fused in the alchemy of commitment.

SAY GOODBYE

When do you say goodbye?
Did she leave the day she said,
Who is that man that brings me breakfast each day?
I said that would be me.
No, she said, that other man who lives here.
No other man lives here, just me.
What is that man's name I asked.
The next time you see him ask him.
I bet his name is John.
Just like you she said
Yes.

When do you say goodbye?
Not when you see her eyes
Frightened into an acknowledgement of decline
Eyes dilated into a frightful stare
Understanding what is happening
Understanding the end result approaching.
You don't say goodbye,
You hug and comfort, pour your energy into
The circle of respect and support.

When do you say goodbye?
Is it the vacant look into the nether world
The look that ignores all of this
Ignores that which surrounds
Sees a world of nothing in the future
The eyes empty of cognition
Unable to ascertain the realities of now
Unable to draw connections to people and places.
Her eyes focused on scenes far away.
She is dying. She will die.
Good bye my love

WATCHING THE SUN SET

I was intent, silent, on the sunset
Until her shadow crossed my eyes
All I could see was her waiting for an answer
Could we be?

What do you need, I asked, voice subdued
Trying to address the questions that lie between us
Attempting to find a path

What I need is to know if you are the one who will answer the call?
She replied. Can I count on you?
I tried to look through her and said I don't know
You demand so much
Let me watch the sunset right now

She insisted, will we have a future?
I don't know, I replied
Let me watch the sunset,
Look, the clouds are changing
From white and gray to red and orange
Golden in the late afternoon.
I'm looking for the secrets in sunsets.

Who do you think you are? A sunset!
Do we have a future or don't we?
What is your problem?

The problem for me is you and me.
I need to watch the sunset right now,
I need to figure out the sunset.
I need to figure out us, I have my doubts
Let me watch the sunset,
Let me see what I can see
I want to see the explosion
Of color heading to black.
Then I saw that the end of the day was
My relationship with her mocked by nature
    in the progression of time.
    A splash of color followed by the night.

She turned away, took a look at the sunset and said
So that's it? That's the way it's going to end?
    You have doubts?
        What can I do?

Do what you think is best.
I need to watch the sun set.

TABLEAU

I am immersed in flora
Trees broadleaf and needled
A mixed forest
Varietals unnumbered
Shrubs green, red, and golden
And grasses of varying heights and colors
Some heavy with seed
I am an interloper
Though we share DNA
Our fortunes took separate paths millennia ago
I walk quietly, lightly
Determined not to disturb
This lovely ecosystem.
I wish to be a part of this tableau
Knowing my differences
Yet knowing if you include me you add value
In diversity, creating new possibilities
Inspiring new directions
I treat my surroundings with respect and care
Understanding that I will be treated with respect and care
We will nurture the other
So that all will prosper and grow.

MESA VERDE #11

Peace,
    Power,
        Quiet,
Mortarless stone russet in the fading light
Piled proudly once into homes and towers tall
    Square
    Round.

Houses
    Echoes of homes
        Dreams of dreams
    Women with mano and metate
        Cooking corn tortillas
        On the roofs of kivas
    Silent, secret ceremonies
Down the ladders below

Spirits are here
    Flowing through the pinon and juniper
    Through the walls of stone
        Up cliffsides
    Across forgotten fields of maize
        And squash and beans
Edging into the world of thought and conscious regard.

Brothers and sisters, mine,
Lived and reproduced here
Disappeared for centuries
Yet still inhabit the silence
Whispering noiseless requests
Within the wind

Stay.
Be one with us in perpetuity.

TOUCH

Will you touch me?
Kinetic, psychic, emotional?
Will you touch me?

My shoulders ache in the aging of the body,
My knees scream their disdain for the life I have led
And my hands roar their discontent.

This body has boldly stated its ongoing conflagration of agitation
With the years of abuse, the lack of care,
The onerous ritual of sport, disregarding the tendons and cartilage.

Working within the confines of evolution,
The choices made when the body was young, the aches and injuries,
All part of the stretch of the psychic denial of age.

Part and parcel, packaged discontent with growing old.
There is no receipt for that which was offered,
Given in the moment, the beastly intent.

My body reflects the numbing decisions to persist,
To deny the limitations of the blood and the tears,
To walk, to run, to exhaustion, to succeed

Will you touch me?
The shell that has emerged from youth,
The figure that stands erect in the courtyard.

Will you touch the me that is me?

TIME OVER TIME

In younger days saturated in sunshine,
triumphant with testosterone,
vibrating in tuneless musicales,
the future was measured in lifetimes
an eternity of tomorrows,
Into limitless expectations where time was always enough,
more than enough to accomplish a life of triumph.
Time was without bounds,
Forever
existed in those buoyant days.

Younger days,
feverishly consumed life everlasting
frittered, as only a limitless thing can
amid the casual excesses,
the daily exuberance, yet
recognition bubbled through nights of neglect.
The mirrored visage of shaved mornings and showers,
eyes shot bloody,
dawning reflected futures.
Leathering skin launched cognition that lifetimes are circumscribed.
bounded by forces inevitable,
forces compulsory.
Amid shivers and jolts,
goose bumped awareness.
limits at some outer edge unrefined, become real.

An "end" is out there somewhere.
Ripening daily,
realities redefine,
lifetimes are reduced to decades and a number exists,
A number designating what might be left,
what might be the limit.
but decades are still the measure,
still time enough
to grow old.

Decades are consumed in fugitive moments.
Pin-striped and tied with silken knots,
Italian shoes and golden chains,
Suburban colonials,
yards and flowered gardens,
SUVs and color TVs
Wines sniffed and swirled, spit with pleasure.
All necessities in the life of a life
In the pursuit of a passage populated with things,
crowded with possessions.
Still time seemed enough.

Decades decay through the withering of years,
and they did.
Time shrinks in capacity.
Suddenly,
is there enough?
Is time running down?
Is the spring unbound?
Time becomes cramped and paltry
as decades become years,

still a number large,
but not so large as to ignore.
The boundary impinges perceptibly;
that frontier fencing the future,
finitely.

Years disassemble, one and another,
Linked chains of milestones,
birthdays,
anniversaries,
funerals,
but always a terminus appears.
Years become meaningless,
crowded with unasked questions still unanswered.
I begin to count seasons as they come
A winter warmer than most,
a spring of storm and snow,
a summer of shadeless heat,
leading shameless toward fall.
I, caught in the negligence of seasons,
hope for one more and another to experience
the limitless cycle
that lies outside the existence
of mortals.
There is no investment in time,
only withdrawal,
drawn to the account of experience.
Choices are made,
Solstices, equinoxes, moons new and full
shine and dissipate.
We cannot add to their total,

Only experience that which exists.
Time encroaches as frets and worries occupy our days,

The changing of the skies, blue to slate gray,
the kindling of the summer,
the wind shifted north and cleverly cold,
Leaves browning and gold,
chlorophyll flushed into the rapidly waning days,
color sucked into the coming frost,
banked in root and seed
Another springtime will come in time,
but will there be time?

I will someday squat in the glass paned warmth of the sun
That will separate life from me;
sit within the manufactured summer of green houses,
watch the liquids drip clear through
plastic tubing coupled to veins.
Time willfully mutates to months,
maybe weeks,
an ending in the path will be palpable.

Not far off,
that bulwark on the horizon,
will amplify each moment.
The years
The weeks,
so full of hours,
will tail into days,
Each notched on the handle
of the walking stick that I will hold.

Days,
whose notches will not reach the top,
days numbered too few and I will realize too late
there is not time enough to undo
what I have done.

Days will be parsed
measured in hours,
blind opiates and chemotherapy
eating at the wreckage.
The time that is left,
consumed in great gulps of pain
Where pieces of the detritus will be gone from memory,
from experience,
Left in the voids between the minutes,
but not yet,
not erased today or tomorrow.

There will be a brief future where time will compress
to minutes
and then seconds,
Where each breath becomes the metronomic will to exist.
One more twinkling.
But it is not yet,
and the course of the days must play out,
but not as in the past,
Where the duties of selfless subsistence
supplants the will to live in glorious moments.

There is time yet,
if it is not squandered,

Not predetermined in mindless projections of destiny.
Time is what is and might be.
Why,
during the mitochondrial lifespan of the self
do we insist that experience must be sheltered,
psyches protected
and mirages of truth honored?
Why do we not lead a life of trial and error,
A life of the possibilities,
devoid of the fears that envelope us
the guilts that stain the soul
the denials that society dictates in the sanctity
of bedrooms and tea houses,
The societal recriminations of right and wrong?
Some days exist
if they are not humiliated,
in the superficiality of
plastic relationships with family, friends, and cohorts
that foster ownership of spirit and will.
Create a life of experience,
of trial,
a life of error in trying.
full of terror and love,
replete in commitments and detachments,
what ifs.
There is time,
maybe not time enough,
but time exists to begin a further volume of life.

What is the life that will satisfy you?
Is there space in the continuum of existence
for the uncertain,
the tender,
the profane,
the almost that is and might be?

Let us,
you and I,
sate the chance given,
seize the opportunities afforded to touch,
to probe,
to discover the aegis
of this lifetime,
the entire lifetime
that has been afforded.
Let us,
you and I,
experience what we should and can with the other.
We can start where time exists purposely,
each moment exists for us.

Meet me for coffee and sweet rolls,
will you?
Will you meet me?

THEY ARE HERE

They are here
Various colors and shapes each bringing
Varietals of humanity
A polyglot of souls
Meshed together into a cacophony of spirits
Around a vast playground, a wilderness
Replete with bloodshed, heartache
Can we see them individually, striving
Or merely as a grouping, an amorphous lot
Of souls in movement
Across a wasteland of hopes and expectations
Grasping for one and another
Looking for connections
Searching for survival
Who will sort out the future of the
Dangling people at the rope's end
Clutching the vision
The dreams and hopes
Facing the reality of their existence
Searching for the helping hand
Searching for a life and a future
Will we assist or
Will we allow the winnowing of futures?

THE FOG IS LIFTING

The fog begins to lift in slow motion
And what appears to be a path is sensed through the hazy mist
Sodden limbs of wondrous trees bend low over the path
Creating a bower that has kept the path dry

Is that a person down the path
Just at the edge of perception?
More a shadow than a figure
Unrecognizeable in the half light
Yet still it seems to be someone tangible
Waiting beneath the overhanging branches
Waiting for what purpose? For him?

Farther on a neon light shines yellow
Illuminating the murky clouds around it
Casting a hollow of muted light in the clouds
Revealing what might be a wooden gate
Thrown open in the stone wall
That borders the path
Suggesting an opening to another
Dimension unseen behind the barrier

A tingle flows up his spinal cord
Hitting his brain with a message
"Take a step you fool, this might be the way"
What lies beyond the path is clearly unseen
And doubts about the future
Have not been resolved
Doubts of the path's intent swirl.

He takes a deep breath, stands tall and
Takes a step onto the path, then another
Somewhat tentative but purposeful and thinks
I guess I will find out shortly
Who or what is waiting and why.
He starts and says
We'll see.

WHIRLY-GIG

I sit inside a whirly-gig
Watching scenes of my life whiz by
Family and friends, parties and dinners
Games with trophies attached
Teachers who inspired or tried to restrict
Lovers who loved or tried to control
Scenes fly by and
I, attempting to find meaning
To understand that which has happened through time
Focus on minutie that would seem to be unimportant
In the grand scale of a life
But always seemed to switch the balance
A life proceeds in narrow deflection
A word here, a deed done, a pat on the back
In the most opportune time
There are people who in the moment needed
Provided what was needed
And I stand today in the fervent desire
Hoping that I too have provided
That word or that deed on some occasion
That helped another to move forward
I am the recipient of many in the scenes
Flashing unremittingly in the whirly-gig
Hopeful that others find me in their whirly-gig
Someone who helped them to succeed
And catalog positive scenes
In their whirly-gigs.

WORRIES

Worries had infiltrated his mind
Little silver spirochetes of unease by the dozen
Gnawing away at self-confidence and belief.
They chew the fabric of resolve
Leaving holes in the psyche and the personality
Limiting the ongoing search for meaning in the last years
Threatening the survival of the self.

Worries created by the ongoing charge into old age
The unrepentant plunge into the elderly
Bodies in disrepair, aching and throbbing with pain
Memories shaded and lacking definition
Recalling a struggle to maintain
Words lost in transit, broken neural chains
All part of the destruction of the self.

Worries compile a notebook of overlooked priorities
Regrets and disappointments compiled over time
Wishes and yearnings left unresolved
All part of the fertilizer of need feeding the spirochetes.
How can one repair the damage that has been done,
Repair the lost focus on fulfilling the future that is left?
Some chances have been lost, some effects permanent.

With great resolve and a chastened encouragement
Some growth can be found,
Some sense of destiny restored.
Worries compel action, direct response, a rejoinder
To the encroaching negativity of life.
Can it be found in the daily routine of survival or
The outlandish display of the unique to squash their intent?

You've got to be tough to age well, so
Fight, battle, confront and always keep your head high.
Do what can be done to resolve worries.
When there is no resolution
Accept and then accommodate.
Worry is a worthless little beast best dismissed.

SUNSET

I watched a sunset for the first time in days.
It is a pink and orange and blue tableaux of ancient times
Created to remind us that the world still creates wonders
Each time we listen to the wind
As the sun slowly slides behind the horizon
The colors are splashed across the sky
Tinting clouds into wondrous creations of sight
Expanding across the remnants of the day
Until that instigator of color disappears into a starlit night.
I, watching the transformation am anxious for the morning
To see what the sun will provide
Bookends of intensity splashed across all that can be seen
Attacking eyesight
pupils dilated to accept the bounty

PRIORITIES

One learns through aging the signs of importance
The place assigned for connection by one and another
The concentric circles of relationship emanating from the heart
Like growth rings on a tree people are assigned to a ring
Based on their importance.
Those closest to the center, the heart, most important and
Moving outward less so.
Family close,
first in line when time calls,
available at a moment's notice
Friends held dear,
singular in the attention given to those
And those further from the core,
assigned lesser status.

She will say, Let's see if we can find a time
He will be there when he is available
The cataloguing of friendship into tiers of connection
Determines the importance of the connection
He, she, will be there when needed when it is
Convenient within the prioritization of the relationship
There is no fault in this,
it is reasonable and necessary
To categorize relationships,
not all can be primary,
Or secondary,
or tertiary,
or some other ary.
We all schedule our contacts within the constraints of time
Within the constraints of need.
Within the parameters assigned to each
Priorities exist and they are obeyed.

LAST STAR

I saw the last star
Flicker a semaphore
Through black cloudy wastes
Ink spots of sky against the cosmos

I saw the last ember
Wink defiantly red
From ashen and pale faces
A toothless smile in duskiness

I saw a glowing, gleaming cat's eye
Blink shut, open, then disappear
Beneath ferns and flowers
Silence trapped on a mosquito's wing

I saw me, shackled in prayer
Calling warnings that were absorbed
Noiseless into humdrum, humdrum
A dying man amid smiling mourners

REMEMBERER

I am a Rememberer
A teller of tales left out of time
Without tribes of innocents
To listen and learn.

I have the origins of peoples
Locked within
And the demise of gods
The history before the tides of man
The emotion of species gone.

But there are no campfires
Wide-eyed faces clutched tight about them
Eager to hear of other moon sets
Long forgotten
Save by the Rememberers

The last embers have whitened to ash
They give no comfort
And the stories are gone
From this earth
Left to fly through the cosmos
Searching for an eager ear
On alien shores.

FRIDAY

BRIDGES AND ROADWAYS

She built him bridges from the day he was born
A great erector set of emotions and thoughtful reactions
Taught through her example,
That he could use to diminish divides between him and others
She constructed pathways of caring
Roadways of empathy through her daily
Interactions with others
He watched, unaware of the impact
Her behavior would create in him until
He became a man of character
A man of substance because of her
Realized that she had built wondrous pillars
Of thoughtful consideration, openness, and acceptance
Taught without saying what he needed to do
She modeled the necessary each day, each interaction.
He thanked her for the gifts she had given him
While she lay dying in her bed
Gave his appreciation of her lessons
He is the man he is because of her.
She raised her right hand gently
Touching his arm and said
I really didn't do anything special
I just tried to do the right thing

Her hand fell to the bed as
She fell into a coma
And then into hospice
Each afternoon and evening's visit
He told her the day's events
The successes of her grandchildren
His struggles and triumphs
And her heart continued
Her spirit did not depart
Her body withered but that great heart
Continued to beat
He began to wonder what he had forgotten to say
To keep her here like this
Then out of the untuned thoughts he said
I have forgotten to say I love you
A thousand times and more
So he did
The next day as he approached
The doctor and nurse were at her door
She died while he was gone
Sparing him the pain of watching her go
He took her hand once more

Held it gently,
His thumb massaging the leathered skin
And said one last time
I love you
He continues to build
bridges and roadways for his sons
Who have become men of substance and character.
They will build bridges and roadways for theirs
And her future is assured.

GREY

Grey, undisturbed from horizon to horizon
Unbroken clouds in a seamless dome of uncertainty
No heavenly lights sending shafts of salvation
Absent colors intense that could be
Beautiful in photo and painting,

There are photos to be had for the skilled
Textures found in the clouded sky, divots and wells
Tinctures darker or light if the eye is keen
And swirling suctions of precipitation apparent
For those in tune with the nuance of light.

The search for color in a colorless world goes forth
Outside the ordinary realms of perception
Looking for optic nerves attuned to that which could be
Seeking the unknown colors apparent to some.
Looking for the unseen in the seen.

Tomorrow, it is probable that the clouds will dissipate
Revealing a panorama of unimaginable beauty
A spectrum of rainbow brilliance
Sparkling in the renewal of pigments fueled by the sun
Red, green, yellow, purple, blue in the lens.

Rainbow pageants are easy to capture, bright on the lens
It is finding the beauty in the unbroken grey
That differentiates the master from the casual recorder
The eye that is exquisite in the nurturing of the day
The one who will record the beauty of grey.

CRYSTAL RAMPARTS

Two watchers, wary,
eyeball to eyeball, brown and green
across the ramparts of crystal and silver
the starched linen war zone of their marriage.
Cautious in the dinner's decay as cocktails and chardonnay
take hold of the means of deliberation,
Loose the footholds of restraint.
Conflict manifold during the ripening silence
heralding an armistice's end,
The alcohol-surge of truth
In the martini's rumpus room of speech.

He could hold no more, he feared,
bile rising in his throat
Tongue pushed hard against his palate.
Behind his teeth,
clenched in resolution
words massed in untidy piles.
The barrage could begin at a moment's notice, while,
Escargot sat on china plates unattended in butter and garlic
Parsley a green reminder of fertility
That had withered in the heat of their summer's past.

Shells to lob across the unpeopled expanse,
to smash the bastions of the other.
Shells to hide within, shells to protect and conceal
to shield him from speech,
to stop the discharge
of the sentences and paragraphs filling his mouth.
For if he would speak,
he would speak the truth,
ghastly with venom
And the air would be fouled with malice.

He chose retreat,
A tactical victor without casualties,
no declaration spit or indictment confessed.
He did not speak
left the table in silence,
silent without him

APPRECIATION

Dawning light filters through frosted windows
Framing a silken scene of snow and ice frozen in continuity.
The house next door exhales a thin white cloud of exhaustion
A remorseful remembrance of the winter that continues
Desirous of the sun's return,
the beginning of spring.
It is quiet,
the snow pads tires and feet,
Quieting the shuffle and scuffle of activity renewed,
As the pulse of time begets new explorations in the day's design.
A shovel scrapes in the distance
clearing a path through the snow
The only disturbance in the chilled morning,
Creating a pathway to the regimens of necessity,
defeating winter's intent.
I, sitting by the window,
coffee in hand, reflect on days past
As curls of steam rise,
the wonderful aroma of morning.

It is quiet,
no radio or morning news to disturb the solitude,
No other voice or breathe to share the warmth of afghans
Created by hands no longer here,
hands melted into the soil
Before the land was frozen,
before winter.
Morning light shrivels through skies becoming clouded
Stratospheric clouds,
cirrus,
the ongoing winter's blanket
Diminishing the sun's ability to heat, to heal, to provide warmth.
Clouds slide over the horizon,
streaky, then filling spaces
Creating a scene emphasizing perfection in shades of gray and white.
"It is beautiful" I say aloud to myself,
the words reverberating into nothing
No one present to affirm my judgement,
no other to appreciate the scene.
I should begin to move, I think,
to ready the day,
but decide to tarry a bit longer,
I need time enough to appreciate the scene for two.

NORTH DAKOTA MACADAM

Thunder in the background
    A low reverberation,
    Subsonic waves of discontent,
A rumbling, rolling vibration of displeasure
A grumble of disaffection behind the featureless horizon,
    Beyond the calloused edges of sight
        Beneath the cramped distorted clouds
A sorrowful roll of megahertz drawn in this afternoon.

Squinting before the fading light,
    The light behind facades
Eyes are deceived by distances,
Fooled by the sounds grumbling behind the present
Tricked by the power of storms,
    The echoes of storms,
        The startling thunder,
            The ultra vibrations of life.

Clouds roil into the afternoon,
    Dark and violent,
The hail bouncing in atmospheric hyperbole,
    Growing,
The damage done,
    Unspoken after the night,
        After the lightning
Has flashed a landscape's scene of neglect and affront
Revealing scarecrows in the frightened light.

The darkness of a Dakota evening,
    Alone on the prairie,
Punctuated illumination by the storm's approach,
The flashing grins of August storms,
    Summer's howls,
        Moans of heat,
            Left over from the days,
                Cloudless famines of wet

Disregard the patchy heavens,
    Disdain the guidance of stars.

On a two-lane track of macadam,
    A pathetic path through this world
Lightless in a wheat field womb of remembrance
Lies a portent of two-lane brilliance abstained,
    Onward into mortality
A yellow dashed line,
    Bound for the barren and apathetic,
        To the tilled fields of the forgotten,
            Fallow fields of lost veneration.

There had been warning signs of a dead-ended future,
    A yellowed diamond
    Nailed to a wooden stake struck into the land,
        Ominous,

But Ignored,
    Dismissed,
        Forgotten in the flush of youth.
The sameness of the Dakota grasslands closes round the soul
Yanks present into past,
        Where hearts lay disquieted.

Struggling within the constraints of life,
    The limits of existence
Pushed two-handed into the blackness of prairie,
    Howls of outrage,
        Discontent,
            Splatter into the void
Where the stars absorb anger,
        Stem the fury with life
Where the moon succors,
    As best it can,
        This foul intent.

In that distance,
    Beyond the subtle curve of the earth,
Behind the colored articulated maps of the landscape,
    The flatness of heart,
        Of mind,
        The anguish of the present
Hearts clench in fear and minds knot,
    Tangled anxieties.
Is there shelter from this storm?
                Is there a place to be?

Heaven's light flickers with recognition,
    Flashbulbs of reality
Frozen in the truth of the moment,
    This snapshot of life.
Rapt in obscurity,
    Shrouded in failed expectations
Revealing the solitude of existence,
    The seclusion of thought.
Within the cloistered,
                Introverted,
            Lonely,
    Course of days.

BIRD SONG

A bird sings
outside my window near the balcony
Quavers and twitters but for what purpose?
Where is that bird,
hidden within the confines of the tree, and
What kind of bird is it that sings so melodiously?
I scan the tree with hopes of honoring the bird by identification.
A brief glimpse, it is blue
It seems tireless in its creations and I wonder
Is the song a foreplay calling for sex, to attract another?
Is this the season for procreation?
Is it a celebration of freedom in this luscious landscape
In a tree made for performing
Or just sung for the joy of singing, creating
Introducing artistry on a sunlit afternoon
Singing with no intent beyond the creation of the song?
I sit quietly, fortunate to participate in the presentation
Pleased that the bird has chosen my tree and me

SHEET OF GRAY

There is a translucent sheet of gray, intensely settled in,
A curtain of moisture,
a sheet of earth's tears
Between the foothills and me,
between the rocks of the cliffs
And the leveled lands of society.
Perched on the edge of uncertainty on the edge of the Rockies,
Hunkered in the shelter of my tent,
sitting cross leg in the opening
watching and listening
raindrops beating a staccato rhythm
Dry in the protective niche designed to shelter
I sip scotch from a plastic bottle and eat crackers with cheese.
No other soul is near and the landscape closes round,
Great granite boulders deposited ages ago strewn askew across the hill
The sweet smell of rain-soaked juniper and aspen.
The musical lilt of raindrops regular and alert.
I will sleep well tonight in my bag,
warm through a chilly evening.
Next to my tent, within arm's reach is the coffee pot
Ready for the morning on the camp stove,
breakfast in bed
Alone in the way back,
in the last strongholds of alone
I am ensconced, and satisfied.

I LET HER GO

It is done
I thought it would take longer.
She is no longer the now.
I thought she would linger
A soul who would provide solace.
She left in a shimmering solitude void of sound
The conversation had ended, truly ended,
There was nothing left to say
I watched her silhouette disappear into the afternoon
Light beams bending around her physique
She could have stayed without conversation.
Stayed to salve the relationship
My goodness, why did I let her go?
We didn't need to talk, just touch
Feeding the physicality of life.
She would agree
if not for me
Dictating a conversation she hated.
Searching for meaning in the pulses and pauses
That emphasized the lack of connection
She was what she was
so was I.
Really, what did we need to talk about?
Why did I let her go?

BLACK BUG

A small black bug
Has landed in my wine
A suicidal plunge into a cornucopia
Of sweet temptation
They say that alcohol in excess will kill you
The little guy has proved them right.
He is dead, no movement apparent
I fish him out with my finger
Do pickled bugs taste?
They say bugs are a good source of protein
I will pass on the taste test this time and
I drop his drunken carcass
Into my pot of rosemary on the deck
I do not prepare a little grave and
Do not play a little taps
He will serve a purpose however
Will add to the soil nurturing my herb
Thank you, little bug for your assistance
I sip my wine
He has not affected the taste of the wine
A nice Bordeaux
I appreciate that.

NAKED OAKS

Outside my windows
naked oaks bend to the breeze,
More a nod to the winds of the spring eternal,
Than a haling of the seasons rebirth,
Sketching a portrait of potential,
a picture of what could be.
Leafless,
Pleading for winter's end, and spring's rebirth
They stand ready to flower,
to fulfill the seasonal charge into summer,
Ready to green the firmament with leaf and shade provided.
The sun is replete with nourishment,
a Colorado intent.
I, waiting for the buds to bloom,
waiting for the leaves to form
Watch hopeful for the day of rebirth,
the start of the season,
That will provide,
will succor hope,
will reestablish the ongoing charge into the future,
the prescient reconciliation of time.

Spring will be sprung, summer will be replete, following
The ancient flow into the seasonal transference.
It will occur, and
I, waiting for the change am anxious,
ready to catalogue the displacement of cold,
To the fruitful regeneration of the now,
Am ready to rejoice, to shout,
to exult in the transition to warm.

DINNER

Dinner has been prepared
Served to the only diner,
the cook
Alone in the kitchen with knife and fork,
A single serving cleverly conceived to foster appetite
To deceive the mind and render completion.
Dinner is served on a solitary plate,
a solitary glass of wine,
one for him,
and one more for him.
Eating slowly to savor the preparation.
He watches the stove grow colder,
ponders the clean up
And wonders what he would do if he never cleaned up.
There are leftovers when cooking for one.
There are pieces of dinner that could be eaten again
By another,
but no other exists
Only the solitary mouth of the cook,
who cooks well
And cooks only for himself.
The leftover will reprise the dinner tomorrow
It will pretend that the cook has cooked again
Pretend that the meal is satisfactory.
Dinner will be served.

SILKEN SHADOWS

Silken shadows of silent tongues
    Sketch the scene,
    expand and rove
In rippling voice-blown waves
In slippery,
    silver rustles.

Silent tongues
        delusive, dour
Afraid to gurgle laughs and frowns
    At ladies wearing Da Vinci gowns
For fear that eyes can see and ears can hear.
Silent tongues,
    alone,
        alone,
            alone

No one to protect or save
    Or give shelter from the wave
Of non-said words that envelop and overwhelm.

Silent tongue,
    silent word,
        silent mind
Silence is a deafening sound
    That swirls and rises,
        falls and drowns
Family and friends,
    Man and mankind.

BIRD SONG II

Less than a cupful of brown and red feathers
The finch lands on my railing,
cocks its head,
Looks briefly at me and makes a formal bow,
Flits to the tree by my balcony and
Begins to serenade with trills and swirls of song.
Finch a cappella in my landscape
I applaud quietly the performance,
Appreciate the wonderful dexterity of sound
And the composition and continuous innovation,
My little jazz performer,
improvising and interpreting
Its surroundings and its licensure to perform.
What a lovely beginning of the day.
I am hopeful of a reprise for tomorrow
Yet grateful for what I have received
From my little feathered songster
if it does not return.

WINTER COMES

Winter comes,
it does,
To each and all in turn,
Stealing insidiously down brambled pathways,
Over the stubbled corrugations of wheat fields and corn
Expending rainbows to shadows of silver and gray,
An alabaster coverlet of frost and antiquity,
Unbroken uniformity,
obedient through time.

Yet below,
in the coal seams snaking beneath
Appalachian hills,
Pennsylvania forests,
In the neural reaches of geologic certainty
Outside conceit and conscience
A fire flickers,
fervid scarlet,
sanquine,
In fissures between sandstone and shale,
A fire burns perpetual.

In the surfaced realm of nuded birch and rippled mire
No bruise of smoke or steam extant
There is nothing but the inter-spatial cold.

Autonomous beneath veneered facades,
undetected,
a fire burns
subterranean,
Cloaked in the depths,
in the hidden places,
Of Paleolithic pasts.

A fire burns

THEY HEARD

He and she simultaneous in their meeting
    Detected the breathing of enzyme and virus
    Cellular awareness in their DNA
Pheromones unleashed attacked sinus and cavity
    An inarguable draw to the mainspring
    A change in the magnetic poles of their person
They heard the humming that vibrates
    Behind the tympanic membrane
    The voice that rises from eucalyptus roots
The murmur that flows through the essence of daisies
    Rhythmic within the dance of aspen and pine
    Consonant with the walk of deer
Rising crescendos of emotion
    Swept over them uncontrolled and dangerous
    Italicizing seasons of connection and relation.
Melodious together in the symphonic overture of life.

He and she gasped, grasped, recognized
    the bedrock of nature in their meeting
    an immutable basis of attraction.
Skin sensitive to subtle fluctuation of isobars
    The vibrations incarnate that extend
    From saw grass to serpents to suns
Chains of creation transparent
    Amplified through their joined prehistory
    Links uncountable and attached
Forged star stuff of evolution,
    Reincarnated encounters uncountable.
The echoes of genesis in their convergence
And it mattered,
        He and she were married.

UNSPOILED

Daylight rebels against sodden skies
Facades of tears moist in the saturated morn
Shadows of the evening, remembered in the vagaries of thought
Burning mist from the land,
Revealing an end.
It was the end, the beginning too
Mediterranean in its sunlight
Intense against the cerulean sea
Warm on my skin, sunburned from the seasons
Spent in the company of you.

The lackluster intent of dolphins,
Swimming in the wake
Had moved into the fore,
Leading love into the deep
Where octopi become calamari
And scaleless fish become the entrée
Swimming in a pool of white wine and olive oil.
I feeding in the frostless mornings,
Past the grateful nightfall of sleep
Welcome the fateful footfalls of a steeped kin
To touch my skin,
to ease my pain,
to caress my bruises
To slumber within the witches' spell.

It is enough in that graceless hour
When the split is spilt from the glass
Onto the mopped ceramics of flower and saint
That I am whole in the dankness of dusk
Humidified in the sea's breezes
No threat of asthma'd breath to squeeze the day
Into a sketch of life,
a struggle with life.
I am alive
That is all,
and that is nearly
enough.
Free of you,
Stretching this rootless peace
Beyond the comprehension of now
Into the unsoiled experience of tomorrow
Preserved for the taking,
no canned experience
Sweetened with milk flowing from breasts unstirred
By struggle, by discontent.
Striving for selfless fulfillment in the life of a life.

CLOUDS

Look! a rhinoceros head, a galloping horse
Do you see it right there? Yes.
What do you find in the clouds above our heads,
In this sculpture of moisture.
A first basemen stretching for a throw
Where? of course, there it is, my young first baseman,
Right there above us in the sunlit sky.
And what else is in the clouds my son?
A dragon chasing a goat?
Where is that? oh yes, how could I have
Missed that tail and oh the poor goat.
We spend time laying on our backs
Spread eagled in the grass
Our dog lies in the grass nearby
Her nose pressed into the conversation,
A part of the day, connected
The lawn in need of mowing,
Maybe tomorrow, but not now, for now
We are investing time for the future
Finding the importance in nothing
And of everything.

THE GIANT IS TURNING

The giant is turning, the tree that covers the horizon,
Patches of gold in the upper reaches of leaves
A bit there and a bit nearer the middle
Is the season here my friend?
Are you signaling the official end of summer
The transition from the wonderous
Summer of shade and green that you have provided
My floral friend has recognized the change
The cornucopia of summer is ending.
I am not ready for the change
But there is no choice
My leafy friend you are the arbitrator
You will signal the change
Without regard to our wishes
It seems the time has come, no reversals of fortune
I need to adjust to the next season,
Autumn is arriving with all the colors it can bring
We accept the natural flow of the days
With winter over the horizon, in wondrous detail
We will be savoring each season as it arrives
And paying allegiance to the flow of time.

HOW ARE YOU

They ask how are you
What do you say?
The truth?
Or the pedantic homily of reassurance.
I am doing well,
I am adjusting,
I am healthy.
Not,
I am alone,
I share meals with no one,
I am rootless, attached to none,
I am cared for arbitrarily
And yearning for attachment to another who desires me.
Evenings progress through solitary dinners,
Watching the snow fall outside the windows
Amid glasses of wine to infiltrate the night.
A lifetime of living alone in the company of others
Has prepared the response.
What could,
would,
they do if the answer was truth?
So, how are you?
Great.

COME WITH ME

Come with me she said,
to where the souls are born,
to where life comes mewling and bawling under the sky.
Come with me,
to where you dare not go,
should not go
to where the visions of creation unbridled will swallow you,
and the barren breast,
silver in the moon will alter your vision,
will bring you to the sweet milk smells of birth unchanged.

Come with me she said,
to where the clear, chastened liquid,
slides burning and honey down your gullet,
where the pure waters harbor the brain's demise
in cartoon's frames of skin and hair,
drawings
of the liquid persuasion that she brews,
Between her silken legs,
her pouting breasts,
her sweet lips.

Come with me she said,
and he followed to find the answers.
He went to the edges and the margins.
He went with eyes wide open and memory erased,
to view the majesty of her,
her slice,
her wanton window.
He followed witless,
a ludicrous lunatic
rejoicing in his demise,
his bloodless extinguishment.

THUNDERSTORM

Lightning all around near and far
Flashing from cloud to cloud
In and about the gray layer
Jagged streaks of electricity.
Thunder continuous providing the percussive accompaniment
Limbs and leaves in disarray through the windblown afternoon
Twisting and turning, diving into the fractured air
And bouncing back joyously
A rousing tarantella celebrating the break from heat.
There is rain in this parched landscape.
The rain dance has worked.
The smell of moisture on the air
After so many drought plagued days lifts our spirits.
We all, plants and humans, need a drink
I lift a glass in honor of my floral friends
To take part in the celebration as I move to safety
The flashes and explosions are too close
The celebration too intense for the moment.
I raise a toast to the thunder storm
Even in its excesses.
We like the exuberance in renewal.

HE KNOWS

She sits on the edge of the sofa
Slides silently toward him
presses gently into his body
Leans to kiss and they fit together seamlessly
Her tongue slides lightly across his lips
And his hands flow easily down her sides
Around her back pulling her gently closer

She is a recapitulation of adolescent angst
A remembrance of backseat encounters
Exploratory embraces,
noiseless kisses
All within the knowledge that boundaries,
borders exist,
Limiting the future,
nullifying the next steps
To ensure that emotions stay safely bottled.

Roadblocks have been established
Flashing lights,
guard dogs,
metal gates secure.
Weathered fences have been erected
Surrounding her homeland,
protecting security
Protecting the life of a life.

She keeps her foot firmly on the brake
Swinging around corners of emotional uncertainty
Always in control,
averting threats.

He,
a scarcely willing participant to the treaty
That defines the terrain,
the parameters'
Aware of allure and discontent,
Is bound by honesty,
allegiance to a code
That does not challenge her described intent,
Honors her decisiveness
Yet is frustrated by the nearness and yet the distance from her.
He knows the reality of the now,
the choices made,
He knows the limits compressed in time.

He knows.

THURSDAY

BARQUENTINE SAILING

Barquentine sailing through the Faeroes
Slipping the straits
Heading for sea.
Westerly winds billow
The silken threads of the
Unblinking passenger
Ruffles the beards of her puppeteers,
Dives through the bellows
To the bowels and out
Reaches the farther side of anonymity
Reaches the soul power extant

She breathes lamentations
Through her nose
And cringes midst the throes
Of unrequited love.
Winces and minces
Toe dancing midst the silver loops of love
Playing for time
Despairingly out of tune
An oboe clutched to her chest.
A muse in disuse.

He a Freudian
Catalogued between fear and envy
Is an encyclopedic reversal
Of the ascent of man,
A beastie
Conjured in the might dreams
Of foolish, foppish libertines.
He exists in the eye
In the palm
Pinched between finger and thumb
A sapphire, a ruby,
A glint in the orchid
That adorns her windblown mane
He exists,
If at all,
In the memory banked,
Found fraudulent,
Bored and stored against early demise

The barquentine sails four masted to the sea
A silently sliding ship
Within horizonless spheres of fog.
Motionless on decks delicate with dew
Gripping the brass rail, she ponders
White knuckled and shivering.
Neither fish nor fowl
Punctuating the featureless void,
The nullity.
Nothing excepting the marks of questions
The answers none may fathom
Crowded aboard the barquentine sailing

HE KISSED HER TWICE

He kissed her twice
Once on the cheek
Once on the lips
She pulled back, eyes wide and smiled
She kissed him back, hard on the lips
Her tongue sliding into his mouth
His hands slid quickly down her sides
Pulling her into him
Clothes evaporate
Into the ether
And the time-space continuum cracked
Leaving a limitless playground
Of orgasmic possibilities
Psychic and personal
Physical and spontaneous
The night progressed into their future
Melding into a joyous coupling
Together

MY FAIRY GODMOTHER

I sit slouched sideways across the bench in the park
When a voice backlit by the sun
Tells me to sit up, and I said what?
She is standing in the grass across the walk
Sit up, she said again. I want to sit down and rest.
Sit over there, I like where I am, I replied.

You need me to sit next to you. I have seen your eyes.
Sit up, she commanded and I sat up.
She sat down close to me, not touching
But an insinuation of contact that was palpable
Through the narrow space between us.

Who are you? I croaked
I am the one you need she said. Your eyes tell a tale.
You take the whole bench to keep others away.
You set up force fields that you think protect you,
Don't allow others near.
I am sent to destroy those inclinations.

Sent by whom?
By your Fairy Godmother, who else.
She wants you to be happy, you will be happy with me.
Incredulous, I reply, What kind of fool do you take me to be?
Just the fool that you are, nothing more or less.
I shrugged, quivered a bit and admitted
I am a fool who cannot recognize good fortune,
I miss opportunities and chances others might accept.

Sitting quietly beside me, a breath of a breeze moved her hair
Across her eye, she brushed it back with the back of her hand
Her aura enveloped me, surrounded me
Pushed my defenses into a hopeless withdrawal

It became easily apparent, even for me
Through my crumbling walled emotions, to see
That she was perfect for me, I could not deny the connection.
I sighed, reached a hand to touch hers and we held hands in silence
The connection was complete and I wanted her to know
Everything about me.
She smiled as if she already did,
Leaned near and gently kissed my cheek.
My Fairy Godmother sent her.
Who would have thought?

CLOUDS ON THE HORIZON

Clouds crowd the horizon, frosting the foothills
Wistful layers of white and gray
No threat of storm or lightning
Balancing the afternoon, the sun's intent
There is little moisture in the layer
More an accent to the unremitting blue
Creating textures in the closure of the day
Observing their movements through glasses
Of polarized effects,
Through glasses of red wine
I am convinced of the subtlety of the sky
The secretive ascent of nature
The unwavering charge into the future
Known only to those who will look
Those who choose to look beneath
And beyond that which lies at the surface.

SLIVERED MORNING

Within the slivered morning,
Outside the piece meal night
She is granite and cold to the touch
Adamantine, impenetrable
Beneath the cotton coverlet,
A block of marble on the linen sheets
A human form inside yet to be revealed
She gives nothing in the dark
She is absent in response.
She would defy the art of Michelangelo.

It is a paint by number relationship
A pretty picture afar,
Each color dutifully placed.
But closer in this refrigerator of love
Flaws can be hidden no more.
The prescribed lines not quite colored within
The paint dried and cracking.

Love has no joystick,
Meant to direct and control,
Manipulate and supervise,
To decide events and outcomes.
There is nothing we share.
I shout in real time, my disdain.
There is too much to give

And nothing to gain.
Within the desire of a shared life
Within the craving to give and get
This vacuum of life is too great
This reality of life grates
She is the reality,
She is what is
And it is not enough.

RIBS AND BEANS

I thought I heard a salvation
bell ringing in my ears
A call to greater glory to further survival
But it was only the dinner bell
Calling me to eat ribs and beans, extraordinary
Still salvation of a kind.

The bell tolls for the ordinary, the sustained belief
That the daily partaking of sustenance is crucial
The survival of the self in the ritualistic creation of the day
Free from the nagging wants and what ifs.

She offers coffee, no cream, no Irish whiskey,
A simple cup of warmth on the edge of despair
Designed to hold in one's hands, a warmer outside and in,
A fragment of the life unstilled by strife and revolution
A drink prepared in quantity for the mass
But adequate for the survivor, alone in the quay
Amidst the multitudes.

The bell rings, and echoes in the tethered existence of flight
Leading lost leaders to the warmth of tomorrow
Within the unsheltered existence of today.
There are beans,
some ration of meat,
and rice
Cooked over fires of broken tiles and railroad ties
in the lonesome world of want.
I was offered salvation,
and took dinner on a tin plate instead.
I will be saved.

TREE

There is a tree across the way
Monstrous in its capacity to fill the view
Arms and legs and appendices
Draped across the block
The Mother of green,
The Auntie of shade
Smiling with the certitude of its place
Knowing the importance of permanence
In a world of change,
Uncertainty.
The tree shoulders this responsibility with grace
Projecting safety and durability,
Stability.
It has lived lifetimes and persists,
Extends its graciousness to all.
We offer our thanks,
Our appreciation,
Knowing the tree exists in time,
In space,
For us,
So that we will not forget
That tomorrow will come,
A new day,
Replete with opportunities and chances.
Connection. And Continuity.

UP WALKS THE BLUES

There I was,
Just ambling down the street
Minding my business,
Keeping my time.
Kicking a bottle top with my feet
Trying to score if you know what I mean.
When out from the alley full of smiles and bonhomie
Walks the Blues like a friend of old
Reaching to take my hand,
To kiss my cheek.
When the next thing you know
I'm sitting on the curb,
Gravel up my ass
Waiting for a dime to roll my way.

I was sitting there with my beer,
Sipping my brew,
Minding my thoughts,
Watching my eyes
Making some time with a fantasy,
Creating some times to savor
When the Blues walks up
And throwing her arm around my shoulders
Gives me a hug,
A squeeze,
And a pat

When the next thing you know
I'm slouched in the gutter,
Piss in my pants
Waiting for Godot to stroll on by.

Well, there I was lying in the sun,
Steaming in the shine
Composing in the sand with my feet
Drawing to a straight with my toes
Pretending to know what I don't
When up from the ocean like Neptune's daughter
Rises the Blues
And greets me with a wave
That erases my meanderings,
Leaves only me
With sand up my ass and seaweed in my ears
Which didn't seem right
But it was all that was left.

SOCIAL MEDIA

He was a watcher of others
Perched in his temple of superiority
Monitoring the unkempt lives of them and those
Cataloguing the daily mistaken decisions and directions
The foibles and faults
Measuring their lack of judgement
Their stupidity, their cupidity
Muttering aloud to himself
As he judged and rated
Through his distorted moral lens
Spewing his thoughts to one and all
He was a watcher of others
So much safer
So much more protected
Than looking in a mirror.

GODDESS

A goddess spoke to me
I saw her moving toward me
A silken slide across the room
Green eyes focused on my face
Her hair glistening in an auburn haze and her
Silvery satin dress, strapless
Caressing each curve as she moved
Her curves were remarkable

Any bravado of confidence crumbled
As she stopped in front of me
Locked my eyes in an electric connection
    Hello, she said.
My tongue and teeth tried to coordinate
    I managed Hello.

I saw you standing here on the edge,
Not really engaging, why not?
Not my kind of thing, I replied
Talking about ridiculous topics that have no substance.

Then why are you here?
My friend Eunice insisted, she wants me to meet people.
I know Eunice what a great lady and
Why does she want you to meet people?

She thinks I can write, she says I write well and
wants me to connect.
I write she said. Radio, TV, newspapers
    That kind of thing.

I'm not published yet, but striving.
I write what I see and often what I see is not seen by others.
I couldn't help myself and said
Why are you talking to me?
There are so many important people in this room.
Why would a goddess care? I asked myself quietly

I saw you standing on the edge.
I like the edge. You have a story, maybe I can tell it.
I don't need someone to tell my story,
    I will tell my story.

And if no one sees your story what have you said?
We all need help at times, I might be your help.
Why do you write?

Is she the goddess who will anoint my head
    Propel me into a new existence?
Should I trust in the Eunice effect?

I write because I must. I said
    I write because the words,
        the visions,
            the dreams

Must be expressed.
    They cannot be contained.
I write so words can demonstrate the substrata
        Of emotion,
            of connection,
                of lives lived in conjunction.

I would like to see your work she said and touched my arm
Would the goddess approve, find my writing acceptable?
Will my words be heard,
    even if the goddess finds them flat?
I was at this party and a goddess spoke to me.

NOT BLUE

Blue yet not blue in the waning day,
A color that replicates the ongoing hours into night
A transition to black
Oncoming as evening infiltrates the strata
The full moon's influence in its tethered existence to science
The physics of attraction and repulsion
Is understood in the illumination of the reflected sun
Shining as a smiling buffoon of light reflecting
Into the atmospheric filter of existence

The source of the differentiated light from abroad
That groaning orb of endless explosion is
Evidence of the fractured bounce of sight in life.
The night borrows the substance of light,
The particle of light
Established in the ongoing sub atomic experience.

A wave of light
Or a particle of subsistence
Is manifested by the creator
In the glorious origination of the day
There is creation, negation, all that can be compressed
In the corrugated electronic background
The unnerving wavelength of reality untouched.

Black yet not black through the night
Bespeckled with pin pricks of light ages old
The dawn of the cosmos illuminating the sleepless hours
The restless ruminations of a slaked evening
Worried that black will become black complete
Fulfilling the genetics of heritage
In the quiet erasure of time.

We wait breathless for the blue projected by the sun
Through wakened awareness, thoughtful projections
Of the day that we love.
Blue can be blue,
Can be pured by the surrounding sighs
Of purposeful people in search of the truth.

ON DIVORCE

A ring of residue encircles his ego
The high water mark
　　When his soul was sound
A saline border rimming his aspirations
Defining the flotsam left after the flood.

Behind the jumbled wreckage of oak and Chevrolet
　　Splatters of rosy silt,
　　　　Streaks of salt sweat about his gills,
　　　　　　　　Resting fitfully amid the
　　　　　　Innuendo and half-truth,
He lies in waiting.

The Alberta Clipper,
　　Frozen,
　　Roars from the pole
Driving migratory icicles to the equator's belt
Siberian blasts,
　　Crash into fronds on palms
Hummingbird nests smashed into the sands

Axis shifting,
    The sun rises in the south,
Continents sink,
    Groaning in disbelief
        Beneath blackened waters,
            Defeated
A sense of immortality denied after a moon of promise

He lies still,
    Latitudinally across the track of man
        Filling the gulfs in the graphs with his ennui
            Filling the time-space continuum
With beginnings that end
    Endings that are doomed.

He lives eating his soul,
    A hobo boiling his shoes
        To tenderize the palate,
            To nullify desire
Consuming his fire,
    His marrow spread across
        His lips,
            His nose,
                Bridging his loss.

Clouds pile in hydraulic construction across the known world
Rumbling in spectral grays
    And even darker thoughts
        Transforming the wellness of the day
Creating subliminal realizations of defeat.

She laughs,
    Insinuating her breath,
        Her odor,
Through amniotic walls of pre-consciousness
    Her sight infiltrating epidermal shields,
A ferret in the glooming dark.

She says nothing,
    Never,
        And not again ever,
But she says them well in calliope melodies
    Tunes that rise achingly in chord then dispel,
Spirochetes of wavering sparrow talk.

Like an insidious argument with now forgotten friends
    She palls the bright-eyed smile,
    Dimples the innocence
        Eyes dilate in surprise
            Flesh prickles,
                Crawls
Shivering beneath rusted ideals and decayed desires.

She is here,
    Frosted fingertips and toes,
        A winter's cloak
Her thoughts carried from cranium to cowl,
    Embroidered
Etherized regrets,
    Stilling all within their radius
Pressing apelike on the visage of victory,
    Destroyed.

THIS GIRL

She shaded the sun from my eyes
I focused on what I needed to survive.
My lips were dry, my eyes dilated.
She was a slender woman, not much shade to offer
But she offered what she had.
Who are you? Are you my savior?
Who chose your little frame to protect my person?
She smiled a little smile
Touching both sides of her lips.
An acknowledgement of her skills.
I looked and said
I need to breathe and pretend that all is well
Can you help me?
My hopes are locked on your wellness
You will understand what I need.
Can you deliver?
Again, no answer, a touch of the hand
Near the thumb.
You have all that you need she said.
You are complete.
Do what you need to do. You can.
Then she left, an almost unheard giggle
Trailing behind her.
Where can I find this girl?

AFRAID

She is afraid
A victim of her past, stitched to memories
Scarred by her remembrances
The legacy of a life deferred for another
A life that had little meaning for the self.

She is afraid
That this one would infiltrate that shroud
Find a purchase in the groundwork of her life
And disrupt the carefully conceived fabric of her existence
The castle she has built on the hill.

She is afraid
Of the tiny touches that lingered in her thoughts
The nights of random kisses and repressed emotions.
The controlled existence of distance and presence
The ongoing limits of her measured performance.

She is afraid.
And her fear is comforting, reassuring
A stalwart defense to prevent a recurring
Loss of self in the defenseless silhouette of existence
Preventing a retreat into the nether
A garrison of protection.

She is afraid.

LOVE AGAIN?

Last night, I almost said I love you
In a moment of weakness
A testament to my need, my desire to connect
When that hyper brake in my brain
Said stop you fool
What in hell are you doing?
Do you love her? Is that the reality?
Or do you love the now the connection
That may be real or not.
Wake up son, grab your crotch and
Figure it out.
Don't be the fool.
I love you? Wow!

HEARTLESS

She did not steal his heart.
It was tendered,
innocent and unscarred,
A gift of love,
his devotion,
his fidelity unrefined.
She took it as her due, she did.
She bound it in her chest,
a dowry of commitment,
She clamped it to her with vows and days of birth,
links consecrated and sacred,
enchantments secure.

There was no receipt or exchange,
none was desired.
His heart was offered without covenant or compact,
guileless,
no expectation of return.
And that is what he received,
nothing.
His heart was hers to do with as she pleased,
as it pleased her.
She did not use his heart wisely,
extravagantly wasteful,
if truth be told
but use it she did.

He had sworn solemn, as did she,
That she could count on this windfall of care.

In years of need and despair,
years of sorrow
he came to understand the forfeiture,
the loss,
that hearts must be exchanged one for the other
not blindly given.
He learned they shared only one thing important
They both
cared for her unreservedly.
It was not enough.

His vacuous, punch-drunk soul,
bankrupt of love, impoverished,
quested for caring.
His heart delivered to indiscretion,
Heartless the remainder,
frantically devoid of nurturing desires
Trusting not,
caring not,
loving not,
itching,
aching for substance.
Rootless amidst lava flows,

the barrenness of molten rock
He lusted for a heart,
to fill his void,
his gap,
to complete his puzzle.

He had no heart,
it was clear.
Manipulation led to distortion.
Able only to cheat and to lie
Scrabbling through touches and turns
Descending into a maelstrom of self pity and doubt
Face flat in the muck
when truth overwhelmed him.
He could not take what he could not give.
He could deceive himself no longer,
could not abide his distorted affairs another hour.
He returned to this love
implored that his heart be refunded.
Eyelids fluttering, half shut, she answered,
no,
no,
once given,
once taken,
done.

This contract would not be broken.
She needed his heart to be whole,
to be of value.

Staggering through fitful existence,
struggling for commitment
that he could not offer,
questing for conscience
In a conscienceless subsistence that sought to expropriate,
not share
he careened through society.
His path was graceless, predatory,
he knew.
He engaged in wasteful flagellation of self,
punishing his indiscretions
Despaired in his wallowing grasps at connection
Built barriers to protect the self
and hopefully others.

Within this destruction of self,
the nihilism of self-doubt
the fears that debilitate
a flicker of light fired in the recesses of memory
through the barriers that he had constructed
A remnant of the self that he once was.
A fragment of the boy who had loved
without condition
wholly
preserved in the darkest abyss of self,
harbored from the ravishing.
He considered
as this light grew to beacon
illuminating neural pathways forgotten
he was his own creator
he was the forger of his steel,
he was the builder of his house and his highway.
Within that kernel of awareness,
that seed of knowledge,
amnesty from his sins was granted,
liberation from restraint conveyed.
He guessed that a heart might be reborn,
regenerated,
reformed.

Conscious of his struggle for existence,
the ethics of self
breathed honest air into his lungs.
The breach could heal,
mend,
rehabilitate.
Scar tissue would disintegrate.

Released from self-forged chains,
demonized cells
he smiled,
a thing forgotten,
lost from the Upanishad of self.
He laughed
a foreign jangle that was pleasing.
Nightmares faded to thoughtless remembrances.
He would be ready to give again,
to risk.
A heart reborn within his genesis.
Past was embalmed,
interred,
but not forgotten.
This time he would share.

MY FLUORESCENT FLAMINGO

My fluorescent flamingo
Shines a beacon of pink across the walking paths
A cashmere sheet of comfort
Beneath my windows
I see walkers smiling as they pass
Some give a wave
Some grin and shake their heads
A young boy, 4 or 5, stops and points, says look.
He is my kind of guy and his parents should be
Required to put a fluorescent flamingo in his room
My fluorescent flamingo
Welcomes them all
Providing warmth and guidance
Lighting the walkway, assisting
Their transit after night has fallen
The world would be a safer place
More amenable and cheered
If more fluorescent flamingos led the way

AUTUMNAL EQUINOX

Autumnal equinox
What a beautiful term
Rolling off your tongue
Around your teeth
A lovely descriptor of the calendar's charge
For those astute to seasons
The forewarning of colder days ahead
So glad I live where seasons change
No monochromatic climate year round
Mornings brisk
A light jacket required
Turning into a magical spectrum of color
During the day
Falling leaves floating on the breeze
Multicolored kites in zig zag free fall
My grand neighbors the trees
In preparation for solitude and respite
Design a showy celebration of color
Created to imprint rainbow visions
On eyes that might tire of the bleak days coming
These scenes will endure through winter
When the grays and whites will dominate
Until the inevitable greening of the landscape in spring
Each season is special
Beautiful in its own way
But the autumnal equinox heralds my favorite.

POEM FOR ANNE

Spider's web fluttering in spring breezes
Torn loose from neglected eaves
Ignored through the winter's season
Rain-scented air sliding from mountain
To foothill to plain
Smoothing down boulder strewn
Canyons heralding transcendent rebirth
Bringing fresh rivulets of life
That sweep through dried and cracked
Channels sweeping debris before them

Seasons of the soul
Not bound to calendars Coptic
Loosened from rootless existence
Nurtured, warmed, protected
Until flowers bloom and fruit takes seed

Windows, doors thrown open
Life pulsating through shadow and sun
Fresh washed walks on paths not lately trod
Beckon to me and I move
Nudged gently, but firmly
Looking for signposts and signs
Finding myself instead
Mining my source
Thank you

WEDNESDAY

WROUGHT IRON

She is profiled on the balcony before the buzzing sign
Leans sensuous across the balustrade
A wrought iron railing
Delicate in its rusted permanence
Wrung from the excesses,
Or just maybe
The authenticity of man and woman,
The seduction of the groove and the beacon.
Her breasts push full against the luscious bar
Forcing a gorge of fantasy between them.
She signals welcome
Subtlety nodding her head,
So casual in the crimson neon
That the law, the enforcers,
Cannot testify that she beckons.
She tempts me to come in,
To come,
So to speak.

It is the quarter Latin,
The narrow channels of seduction,
Fermenting flesh,
Music that crawls beneath your hair
Infiltrates cells in the brain and body
Courses down the whole of your limbs,
Jazz and Zydeco,
You must dance or die.

Between the bawdy houses and gay retreats,
The clubs and bars,
All appetites are slaked in the steaming silence.
We have eaten raw oysters from the shell,
Across cool marble counters
Dipped in the cocktail sauce of New Orleans.
We have sampled the wicked,
Peeked around corners stiff with smoke and absinthe
Entered the half-lit rooms of smoldering dreams
Congested with tomorrows.

They are there and here,
Evangelicals, white shirts starched and responsible ties
Anxious on the fringe of possibility
Waiting for church bells to ring vespers
Calling all to salvation or at least to prayer
The church, bless its liturgy,

Lives on within its preternatural focus on death
Its denial of god's gift of life.
There are rules,
Proscriptions,
Dogma
Written in the dawn of belief,
And there are practices that survive
From ages past, dark ages.

We have sampled the church as well,
Explored its credo
Scoured its writings looking for meaning
Beyond to the afterlife
And found that the etouffee with shrimp,
Is far more potent,
More full of spice,
More full of life,
Than the jaundiced teachings of Testaments,
The new and the old.
Focused on realms that man cannot touch or taste
Outside charm and grace.

It is the file' and pepper,
Soft shelled crab,
Sucking the heads of crawfish,
It is the gumbo of Miss Sarah,

Bayou bred
Replete with shrimp and okra,
Chicken and spice,
Chased with the voodoo black ale
And the blood of the rooster
It is the dawn that makes a human,
After a night of loose-jointed rumblings and rum.
It is not the chain of beads,
The noose of the Church
Kneeling in confessionals,
Eating the wafer,
Tasteless and stale on the tongue.

It is the ingestion of heat,
The release in the night
The plastic St. Christopher melting
On the Studebaker's dashboard,
Back seat playgrounds on bayou banks
Vinyl seats that stick to your bottom and your back
In the lovely sub-tropical heaven that beckons,
The sweet Hurricane of fruit and Jamaican rum
Drunk from cups to take
Onto the streets of Louisiana,
The floodplains of the parish
That make the day and night.

Proudly, I take her arm,
Hold the hand of my lady
As we promenade the levee,
Her parasol red in the setting sun,
My suit pinstriped and sleek,
As we nod and smile,
Give a wink and hello.
We sketch the afternoon into evening.
Stretch the fiber of tonight.
I want to taste the nasty salt sweat of life
And not consider the saccharine sweetness of ever after.

Jesus is my friend,
I know it
And he would not care if I fucked tonight.
Jesus is my friend,
I have been told it
And I know he is cool.
He understands,
And forgives,
Unlike the penguins who live in the church,
Untouched by the supple hands of women.

Life is simple,
We drink rum in fruit juice,
Taste stews of sea and shell,
Spiced with the Cajun and the Creole.
We kiss and love,
And in the morning the sun rises
Where there is cafe au lait and beignets waiting.!
What more can a man, or a woman, ask?

JOURNEY

He strode through Martian landscapes,
flattened to horizons obscure
Nearly lost in the swirling dusts and lights,
filtered red,
that filled the air.
Grit gathering in the saliva at the corners of his mouth,
Clenched tight against the gasping atmosphere,
the stifling atmosphere.
Tears ran from his eyes
became muddied raindrops to self.
Crusted with the landscape,
encrusted with failure,
his body tilted into the wind.

He walked relentless until he reached the exile's end,
the red dust no more,
Found escarpments higher than the eye could see,
disappearing into heavens,
Great granite trapezoids of stone
polished bright by storm,
burnished by time,
No hold for hand or foot apparent,
slick in the weathered day.
Yet he continued,
scrabbling up toe-nailed defiles barely discerned

Fingers cracked and bleeding
until the walls had been crested.
Standing on the precipice edge he gazed distant, eyes shaded
Against a merciless sun,
white in the bleached sky,
across a lacerated plateau.
Before him stretched a devil's lair of volcanic waste
Tortured rocks and twisted magma strewn in raged disarray
sharp edged and fragmentary,
to tear away at skin and clothes
and conscience,
bereft of shelter and liquid to quench his thirst.

He started,
what else was there to do,
and the landscape seized him
Wrenching his resolve,
choking his intent,
pounding despair and surrender.
Yet he continued still,
a walking wounded,
barely conscious,

Scrambling down steep sided ravines in tumbling dirty plunges
Then up again in grasping shifting thrusts against the decaying sides
Two steps up,
sliding back,
yet still moving undeterred.

Then spied in the distance,
green and blue sliced through the dogged panorama,
Beyond, on the far side,
splashes of rose and jade beneath the fading sky.
His essence revived,
it was more than mirage.
he had arrived,
he was sure.
Skin worn thin to paper,
tongue lolling from left to right with each step
Hair matted with the refuse of forty years of days and nights
Struggling in the badlands of his history,
he lunged forward with anticipation.

He found the river,
right where it was,
yet the river had moved,
gargantuan.
It flowed in frightful flood,
broiling and stomping through the countryside,

Swollen with the strangled bodies of beasts and birds,
trunks of trees
And boulders,
driven like sheep in a flock to their congregation.
The water so blue from afar,
was gray and brown and red,
Silted from the stolen lands above,
creating earth below.

He plunged ahead,
the clutching water chasing the grime from his body
Cleansing the tarnish from his soul,
anointed in the holy water of contrition,
In the roiling, boiling crescent of liquid,
washing his sins into the delta.
He defied the currents smashing his face and limbs
and will,
Tearing at the remnants of his array,
driving the wasteland to the sea
And when he emerged at the farthest shore
he was clean and whole.

He picked fruit from the trees as he walked,
apples green and red
Peaches umber,
plums the deepest purple of desire.
Beneath the shading lindens and ash,
between the lilac and wisteria,
Grasses heavy with seed caressed his legs,
attending his scrapes and cuts.
He walked easily on flattened terrain,
walked along pathways well trod
Maintaining his directions,
his purpose clear headed and solitary.

She was waiting for him,
as had been foretold,
standing at the edge of the bight
Clothed in robes of safety and security,
robes of civilization and rectitude.
Throwing her arms open to him,
she clasped him to her bosom and led him sweetly
To the shelter of her house,
the room,
the bed,
sheets thrown open to him,
to her.

She bid him enter,
caressed his shoulders and chest,
absorbed his strength
Brought bands to slide over his fingers,
Golden loops to bind him to this place.
Silken shrouds were brought to him,
draped saccharine over his solemn frame,
Fabrics delicate to soothe his wear,
balms for his sunburn and scarring wounds.
Honeyed tea, sweet and tranquil for his throat and tongue,
in silver goblets
And cakes of deep chocolate,
cakes of cinnamon and sugar,
wafers pious,
were delivered deliberate by acolytes vested in scarlet velvet.

He had only to let go,
to take one step,
to unclench his fists,
to succumb.

No steps would be taken,
his legs could not move,
would not enter that bed,
His fists would not be unclenched to accept the golden offerings,
the sweetened treats.
He shuddered,
convulsed
and the robes slid to the dirt,
the tea foamed into the day.
His gaze turned, past the gild and comfort,
past the smooth words and sweet strokes.

Resolute
he stepped,
felt her print,
her constraint,
slip away,
focused on horizons.
He began to retrace each step,
print to print,
to discover where he had been and why.

His journey had begun.

GREEN

It happened overnight under the cover of darkness
With every intention to surprise and awe
As the sun rose, its light filtered through the beginnings
Of leaves, lime green, on the winter's nakedness
Outside my window creating a wonder of color
Fresh on the springtime
The first signs of the conquest of rebirth
After a long and bleak winter of snow and ice
We have waited not so patiently for a sign
Knowing the eventuality of the transition,
The certainty of change
Thrilled with the grinning green's birth
Welcoming the spaces of nurture
There is a lift to my steps as I make coffee to start the day
Savoring the light stained fresh in my kitchen
Sitting on my veranda cup in hand
I stare relentless at the beginnings of leaves
relishing the green, the breakfast of sight
We will finally be reborn,
Breathe the flowering of fruit and
The promise of the future.

FORCES UNSEEN

The wind
striding across the parking lot
is as strong as me,
no stronger
Whipping in unexpected gusts and swirls,
and I
Stopped in animation by its power,
one step incomplete,
one foot up
am immobilized in time
perched on the equilibrium of the morning.
A sudden gust
emboldened in its capacity
grabs at bags and legs and torso.
My coat billows.
Backwards I go, shoved in directions unintended,
Staggering across the cobbled stone
off-center
On the edge of falling
beyond control.
Embarrassed by a thing not seen,
shaken.

Grasping my breath and my balance once more,
I stare defiant through invisible fists of wind
Astonished by my failure
To see
To sense
To know
That which sways me.
The wonder, the wrath, the awe with forces covert,
but tactile,
flows through every capillary,
instructs each cell
with evolutionary knowledge that
forces ghostly but real
scatter my intentions, alter my perceptions
my pathways
in unforgiving moments.
I begin to move again in a determined orbit
circling comprehension
searching in the unseen for clues to you.

GOD'S PUPIL

Floating above the quarry,
crystalline waters undisturbed
Barely a ripple distorting the consummated reflection of God's pupil
Who breathes quarks and muons while
Matching his beneficent smile to the procreation of now and
Gazes on his precision reflected.

Clouds of misty molecules of religion are created
Through his rhythmic exhalations,
his noiseless inhalations
Swelling to overtake and conquer arbitrary thoughts unbidden,
Lazing in the sky above the landscape serene
The perfected perfection of self-awareness.

It is in the recollection of conscience remembrance of choices
That the self becomes liberated from deceit,
Free to dispense with the dreadful recriminations left behind
In the totality of the remade self,
free of stain
Able to soar above normality, to sail into undistorted skies.

God's pupil sees the radiance of star shine
In the breath taken,
expelled and absorbed
As vapors form to promote the health of the psyche
Training the timed emissions to promote lift
Teaching the lungs to consume and reuse the glory.

On a cloudless day of intent,
a sunlit refuge from
Diseased thoughts, worries, cares and inhibitions
God's pupil desires to be stroked, petted, caressed
With loving intent
to mollify ambivalent thoughts
Created in knowing that a future is uncertain.

When God's pupil seeks compassionate relief
He must look inside,
within the structured belief systems
Inculcated since creation,
instructed learnings that internalize
Presupposed senses of right and wrong,
Choices that have been made in rehearsal.

Gods can do these things, can salve the ruptured process
They can make things whole in the begetting of life
Gods can create futures that the pupil cannot but
Gods only exist in belief,
disappear when no
Reverence is offered, no adoration is willingly provided.

Gods must create new means to survive
And god's pupil is the means to a new glory of existence
God's pupil will create new flocks that follow
Will rejuvenate staid beliefs creating new paths of worship
Will become the new beacon,
they hope.

MAN IN THE SHADOWS

A man hides in those shadows
An indistinct absorption of light
Amidst the grays and blacks of his alley existence
Amidst the sifting swirling fumes of affinity.
He dodges sight, delicate, subdued,
Imperceptible but for the toe
Of the oxblood wing-tip
That slides barely into the boundaried light.

The man hides in the shadows,
Fragmented whites behind fluttered lids
Briefly discerned holes in the night.
He seems oddly positioned to move,
poised,
an insinuation of intent and purpose.
Instead slouches deeper into his protective nook
Settling between trashcans and brick.
Scarcely palpable,
a ripple crawls from the puddle at his feet,
A derision of movement,
deficient.

That man hides in the shadows
    Hands clutching tightened lapels,
        Clenched beneath scruffy chin,
            wool in the wet
Mourning what is lost,
    the remorse of memory.
The oiled slick soaks through the sides of his shoes
    Puckered sockless feet,
        numb in the night.
His head rests sweetly now against his cool,
    damp wall
        pillowed in discomfort,
            penitent in silence.
Reconciled to his alley essence,
    a sigh slides into the fog,
        An exhalation of regret,
            supplementing the night.

MUDDY FEET

I felt my feet sink into the mud
Irrigation taking the first steps to a garden
When I stepped felt the splashes
Of mud on my legs
Drops of the earth crawling around ankles and calves.
I need a hose to spray away the fragments.
I can't go into the house this way.
It is good that I am barefooted and easily cleaned
One of those few times you can
Easily get rid of stuff you don't want.
A simple hose to wash it away.
Too bad we can't do that with the other stuff.
The stuff that sticks to your soul
Your heart
Your conscious choices
Made in unforgiving moments that lead
To the neglect of self and the connections to another.
I need a hose to wash away the stains
Of other days
My kingdom for a hose!

BLANK DOCUMENT

It is a blank document,
No statement of intent or discontent
A simple page of nothing that begins the discussion
Of who and when and where.

No words are written, or scribed
No pictures scribbled with crayon or
Brushed with water color, delicate
With hushed tones of aquamarine.

She is a blank document and I,
Unable to discern her intent, her inclination
Only able to foster a shadow of a thought
Will she be the one, or a whim of wishes in the winds.

There is a blank document
Aching for rhymes of reason, thoughts recreated
Written in ancient texts to confuse and please
The placid reader, the intellectual inquirer.

Blank documents carry no purchase
Deceive the envied pursuit of meaning
That vacuums create, leaving only space for conjecture
Leading the simplified response to nothing.

She is a blank document
Inciting thoughtless thoughts in margined spaces
Alone in the interpretation of nothing
Fraught with possibility and maybe not

SHE SAID

She said I love you in a voice softer than a Hawaiian sunset
Words uttered beneath the Maui sun
Vibrant in orange and blue, atmospherics scattered
As the sky turned into a Pacific celebration
Of golden clouds, scarlet sun, and pastel remnants.

She said I love you
And I grasping at the truth of the connection
Accepted her love, the love given
Accepted the proffer, the generosity
That connection brings and complements.
Desired to be loved and love.

She said I love you
And how will you love me?
I love you and what do you bring to love me?
I had the answer
I bring a devotional, a scripture of caring
My undivided attention.

And she said, is that it? Is that all?
Not knowing what else I could deliver
I smiled and said it should be enough
But it wasn't, something else was needed.

She said I love you
I need more, to restore, to nest
You need to deliver more.
What is the rest?
I, needing respite, said I will give what I have
I will provide.

She said I love you
And loving her became the game
Loving her created trophies she could display
A pelt stretched on a pallet
A horned head stuffed on the mantel
A trophy to be admired.
A sculpture in clay, soon to be bronzed
And books of ancient scripture to peruse.

She said I love you.

MEXICAN SANDS

Cocoa colored skin after
One week on Mexican sands
Beside the waters of Yucatan.
She smells of suntan lotion and sea salt
Moving toward the shower.
Sliding out of her bathing suit
A narrow white line across her back
And her small creamy triangle in the room,
Luminescent against her tanned frame.
She flicks the bottom at me with her toes
Laughs and steps beneath the water.
Stretched on the bed,
I am transfixed,
I cannot remove my eyes,
She is flawless.

We walk on the beach before dinner
Zigzag our way down the sands
Tracing the foam and seaweed rim of the gulf
Hand in hand, fingers twined,
Each finger a miracle, long and graceful,
Sculptures of perfection,
Grazing hips as we move.
A coastal breeze blows gently, brushing her hair
Sun bleached from tropical days and salt water.
The day sets in a palette-stretching swatch

Time converts pastel blue to orange then red,
Achieving a star splattered night, moonlit on the shore.
Her hair glows as the night grows,
Framing her face
A Donizetti halo.

We tickle and tease our path to dinner
Talking of her current taste in poets
Me (a very good choice),
Rod Mckuen, a surprise from the past
"Stanyan Street" and "With Love. . ."
The sentiments, the tone, she says
They match her mood with me.
This woman loves me
Though she knows me too well,
Because she knows me too well, she replies with
Fingertips gently on my arm,
Delighted eyes.
I am outside myself, jealous of my self
Incredulous
That this woman could love me.

She is the lynchpin,
The keystone
The jigsawed piece of life that fits
Perfectly and forever into the puzzle
That is the future.
I am lost in visions of paths trod together
Smitten by the prospects of life,
A life in conjunction.
The world is superfluous,
A backdrop for our love,
A green screen projection,
Of our desires and our wishes.
We will build a house of permanence.
The wind will always be at our backs.

BROKEN SOUL

His soul was broken into a moldy nest of structures
1000 pieces of fractured futures
Who can recreate the picture?
Who will recreate the picture?
She tells him she is the one, she will reconstruct
And recreate that which was damaged.
She tells him of her vision of the future
With his soul intact and his person healthy
She will do it
She will be his savior.
And knowing that she is intent he
Realizes that only he can finish that jigsaw
Only he can recreate his ongoing journey
But he appreciates the offer
Smiles
And says
Sure
give it a try.

IN THE DARKNESS

In the darkness, no sight or sound
Fingers slide seamlessly across fluent skin
Lubricated with sweat, a sheen reducing friction.

In the darkness, where moments are uncharted
Time and distance are deterred, deferred
While the shell of the blackness is complete.

In the darkness, fingers see
Create a sculpture of curves and slopes
Vivid behind the optic nerve superfluous.

In the darkness currents of heat
Rise and fall with the tides of love
Flooding the flats of the lonely.

In the darkness, adrift in emotion
Rasping breathe, a simmer of sound
Sensed rather than heard, instinctual.

In the darkness, turning soundlessly
An apprehension of movement within the arms
Until a smile radiates in the black.

PILOT

Joystick caressed lightly in his hand the pilot
Moves in unexpected spaces drawing upon
Emotions little understood.
He forgoes the loop de loops and crazed dives
For long swinging curvatures,
Outlining the boundaries
Where he is contented and safe.
The pilot pretends to know the boundaries of relation
The substantial connection between yaw and pitch
In the industrial creation of a relationship.
The plane swoops and glides,
Smiling interspaces
Looking for a responding grin.
The pilot is aware of his flawed recognition,
The tactile tingling in his groin, a
Recreation of reality attached to a single motor flight.
The pilot caresses the joystick,
Smiles and feels release
From the substantial, the obvious, the onerous
The pilot caresses the joystick

LOW SEASON

It is the low season—
    A chilly cloudless day, devoid of tourists and dollars
        When I stop for dinner near the beach.
Three waiters, maitre D and wine steward,
    skewered in white formal
And me,
    outnumbered at every turn.
        A single serving of frito misto di mare
            a mezzo of vino bianco.
Seated amidst a landscape of white linens and candles lit
    A sculpture in solitaire
    Within this room of abandoned chairs,
        soulless tables
        glistening tiles
            polished to ingratiate light.

A place had been reserved for this only diner.
      No reservation had been required
Settings extraneous have been cleared,
            disappeared to back rooms
Only a plate,
two glasses,
      the pale lemon distortion of wine and
The aqua naturale, the green bottle half filled,
      the only color
            In the blinding dissipation of the day
When I notice again,
      you're not there.
            It is the low season
                  after all.

FRAMED ON THE WALL

I saw your tree
Framed on the dining room wall at grandma's house
Within simple black borders
No gilt-edged leaves.
Fresh scrubbed faces
Staring forever with unseeing eyes
At America in the form of a lens.

I saw you seated upon grandpa's knee
In shirtwaist and bobbed hair
Your smile glowing, your face consumed with glee
Against his stern and determined lips
His countenance set to battle for freedom

A flowered garland about your head at 19 or 20
Innocence and wide eyes on a marriage day
Photographed in black and white
Waiting for my father, waiting for me
Aunts and uncles in tuxedo and gown
Hair piled into piles or cut to nothing

Your roots once sunk in the Italian soil
Transplanted to the clay of Nebraska,
You smile angelic as you hold me,
Mingled, nurtured by disparate bloods
A shocking head of black hair in the sepia photo.

Your eyes smile at me forever from the frame in the den
You are newly arrived, slight but able
Producing people proud and loving
Producing me,
and I
love you

THE SECOND OPTION

She tells me she is not ready,
there are greater needs,
She tells me to be steady,
reliable,
and she is gone again.
Gone too soon,
gone tomorrow
and today.
I am to watch and wait,
the second option,
the maybe of tomorrow.
I am the shoulder to cling to when Gibraltar falls,
The anchorage to return to when the storm is too great,
the foundation of support when inadequacy attacks.
I am the second option.

SWAYING

Everything is moving
Leaves sparkling their reflection of the sun.
Branches leaning,
turning,
following the currents unseen
The smaller trees respond,
waving, pausing,
bowing to that which exists
The huge trees acknowledge the wind with a smile
Allowing leaves to recognize the intent of the currents
Without bending to its will
Sitting in the catbird seat,
I watch pine and oak,
They sway in rhythm and I am swept with them
I move with them in currents unseen.
I sway and smile with the trees.
I observe the day's progression.

THERE WAS AN ENDING

There was an ending—
Not the ending they might conceive
    Between the bookends of an affair.
It could have been the gasping, throat grabbing,
    Spiraling Shakespearean twist into death,
        But it wasn't.

It could have been the palomino's ass, white tail
    Flicking from side to side chasing flies from its flanks
    As our hero rides into the rapidly failing sunset
    Against the Tetons peaked with snow,
        But it wasn't.

It could have been the kiss of a silhouette,
    Across the Hudson river, against the mirage of New York
    Sparkless in the dark, before the starlights of business,
        But it wasn't.

It could have been six-guns drawn on a dusty street,
    A dagger, the handle capped by a skull,
        slipped between ribs,
A draught of poison to appease the gods,
Maybe a hangman's noose as the screen goes black,
        But it wasn't.

There was an ending—
    Quiet in a dust filled room,
        not quite alone, without drama,
Undistinguished in the dark,
    Shapeless in corduroy and cotton
    Lacking definition
Separate,
    Together in a room,
        Taking leave.
            The end.

MAN AGAINST THE MACHINE

There was a colossal dragon breathing,
a thousand-ton-beast of steel and steam
This train on the tracks ready to roll, right now.
Every party needed was on board.
They were all in line,
supportive and subservient,
heads nodding assent,
The women in the night, the men in the welfare lines
knew it was coming,
they could hear the bells and whistles
This train was rolling and none would stop it.

Curiously,
without warning,
out of the crowd stepped a man,
hesitantly,
Shuffling but deliberate,
but only because no one else would.
160 pounds of integrity,
A slight man,
clothed in denim, soft soled shoes,
He stepped between the tracks,
reluctantly but purposely,
almost shy,
His gaze lowered,
fixed on the steel rails beneath his feet.

This man,
so frail,
inconsequential,
gazed at the space before
The path that the engine had not touched.
He raised one hand,
stretched outward,
as if seeking,
compressing the air before him
A salute to righteousness,
to the power of the individual soul.
Quietly,
almost unheard against the astonishment of the crowd
The small man said, voice quivering,
"This is not right."

The crowd vibrated,
thrilled at the sound,
they understood,
Some wished that they were on the tracks,
But did not wish hard enough to join him.
The sides of the tracks were enough,
trembling with the man
Who had stopped the train,
who had stopped everything.
The train would not,
could not move
while the man stood resolute.

They all wanted the train to stop,
All but those who count,
Those who would profit,
those who decide what is and should be,
Those who know the score
and the balance sheets.
They all craved a hero,
an S on his chest,
but it was only him,
Only this tiny fellow who stepped in front of a train,
Only this unguarded man with a denim shirt
buttoned tight under his chin.

None came to stand with the man,
though many were electrified by his presence.
A voice shrilled in support,
in encouragement,
but quickly stilled when the forces arrived.
To be identified with the man,
to stand in his stead,
was forbidden before the machine.
The man stood,
solitary and defenseless.
When they arrived, as they always do
clubs in hand,
They began with a flourish.
They beat him to the ground.
Blows to the kidneys,
the hamstrings,
they beat his knees,
and as he sagged,
they punched his neck and kicked his head.

They beat him in rhythm,
a tympanic ode to authority and obedience.
No one can stand in front of the train,
to stop progress,
To deter those who would profit from profiting.
The crowd could not watch,
could barely breathe,
as they dragged him off,
Yanking heartily when his toes caught on the ties,
still stuck on the tracks.
The crowd dispersed
and the train proceeded to proceed,
undeterred.

IN UTERO

He was forty-three when he learned of his mother's miscarriages
Three potential brothers lost "in utero"
And he wondered what his life would have been
With three other brothers,
Instead of the wind.

He wondered what his mother had felt,
    As the little ones slid away
Into a basin, unformed and unbreathing,
Yet something,
Something she had wanted,
At least he thought so,
Wondered what she felt the second time or the third.

The crones with their chains of bead, clanking and shaking
Holy Mary, mother of god,
Our father who art,
I believe
In rapid repetition,
Clucked their judgement and their knowing
Of the plans of god,
The pre-ordained trials we all must endure.

Beneath the sanitized mirages of hospitals,
Above the non-coffined little ones unable to draw breathes
Lay a zone of emotion choked and sterile,
Squandered thought rebellious and dire
Outside the feeble assurances of the plans of gods.

Life is afforded in the whirlpool genetic,
Women who grimace and bear, men who question and cry.
Answers are buried in cemeteries
Lush with bougainvillea and granite reminders
Life is life,
Death is death,
We move on regardless.

COTTON COAT

Worn women
Shuffle slowly over cracked
Weed clotted walks
Hump-backed against the snow
That clutches tenaciously to brow and chin
Cotton coats pulled tight against rosy cheeks
Print dresses fringing knees
Scabbed from kneeling, scraping
For life, for love, and god
Gray hair falls carelessly, softly
Flapping against aged brown-spotted cheeks
Wrinkled deep in the memory
Of six children, two husbands
And 47 years of working
And waiting
Waiting for it to happen
Wondering what it was
But hoping it would

TUESDAY

VULCANISM

Vulcan, god of fire and bile
    Father of flames and sulphurous clouds of stench
Filling the nose and the mouth with the taste of death
    Great seismic eruptions
        Rocks and magma flung into the sky
        Ash burying dead and living
    Words that strip the skin from the frame
    Cataclysmic breaches that split and heal
        Within the structure of geologic certainty
        About the framework of a life
        Shaken and destroyed
Columns of smoke and ash and fire into the stratus
Splashed onto the day into the night
Blackening the sun and stars.

A colossal aa moves inexorably
    All edges and corners and points
    Migrating merciless across the years
Burying all within the relentless force of impunity
        Unchanneled by conventions or boundaries
    Heedless of prayer or lamentation,
        The crushing and burning of spirit
Awesomely terrible and beautiful
    Within the reach of love

Vulcanism, the tenacious, viscous flow
  Of rock made barely liquid, of form made mellow
    Splashing succulent on inert emotions
Left unprotected in the flow's awful path
  To the sea,
    To see
      That the magma flows hottest
  On the edge of today, the margin of tomorrow
The gorgeous, ravishing trail into commitment
  Where the crust breaks hot with gas
    Base rock formed tenuous as the lava cools
  begetting a platform for our dependency
    Living always on the chasm cusp,
      Awaiting the un-timed eruption
    That will inevitably come
We are Andreas, at fault, and we will pay.

HOWLING

A full moon,
diamond brilliant against the leaden sky
Breaks through the cloud cover
A beacon of light directed at him
and he began to howl
Long low howls of longing,
Searching for connection across the universe
Hoping for an answer from the wilderness
She was startled, taken aback
Looked to see if he was growing hair on his face
Fangs in his mouth,
or claws on his hands
She saw only him, eyes slightly dilated, tendons stretched
Are you all right?
He blinked twice,
turned to look at her and said
I think you will like this restaurant, great Italian
Good she answered, I love lasagna
he nodded assent
It was a strange start to a first date.

MY BABY

There was green grass at your door freshly mown
Pungent in the wet morning,
assailing the senses,
Moist in this summer's sunrise,
fervent in the nose.
You my friend are fresh on the morning's breeze,
Primordial in your connection with the dawn,
Connected to prior days of lust and fulfillment.
A surprise moment of DNA
and cellular inflation,
An inheritance of cells' division
and multiplication
In the rich soufflé of sex in the afternoon.
The sun's intent
in the stifling heat and shine
Is to whither the proclivity,
diminish the desire

And we, wishing for the forbidden embrace,
the moist coupling in the sacred
silken slide into oblivion
Into the promise of the future,
disregard the obvious,
Pretend that boundaries do not exist,
And you, my baby,
are the answer,
the antidote,
the once again
Into the future.

TIME IN THE HANDS

My sister could see the march of time in the hands of gods
Visualize each second in the atomic progressions
Between the swirls and lines,
thumbs and forefingers,
Upon the calloused,
reddened hands of gods.
She could see the panoply of life before her and behind
Discerned her itinerary in detailed extension
Realized the brevity and abruptness,
and could find
No value,
to her,
to any,
in the sweep
of this eternal nightmare.
My sister saw the progression of time as clear as you
Standing in the midday above her grave, standing in this life.
She could see seasons swing
closer than
the breath
of spring
Could see
the wound tightness of her life,
measured and disassembling.

She could see the days, the hours, the minutes,
Arrayed in close order drill,
marching to her doom,
unperturbed.
And what good did it do her
this knowledge,
this vision?
She died
knowing when she should,
but so what?

MY GARDEN

I have planted seeds
Spinach, kale, and parsley early in the spring
Watched them grow fervently, earthly green
Feeding the soul and this life
Tomatoes in the garden lush, ripened on the vines
Crimson orbs of sundry sizes, varietals cherished
Salads and sauce, salsas spiced with jalapeno green and red
And onions, red and white and yellow, to complement the product
Beans yellow and green and snow peas,
When do we eat?
Walking through the garden in shorts, knees brush the rosemary
Into fragrant clouds of ecstasy
The sweet odor of thyme picked fresh sticking to skin and clothes
The lushness of basil leafy and verdant.
We garden, we grow,
we love the soil beneath our fingernails
Feeling the fertile touch of the land.
We are connected to seasons,
watching the telltale times
To plant, to nurture, to harvest, to eat.
There is connection to the past,
the future,
the now

In the produce, in time spent, invested in health
My garden grows,
Nursing my soul
and I amend the soil,
Adding nutrients organic, composted exactness
Nurturing the land and the landscape with my care,
My sweat, my attention, my efforts
And the garden repays my efforts tenfold
It is my garden, my promise, my shelter.

LOST BOY

There is a lost boy searching on the shore
motherless
Shifting in the dunes,
beside the sea,
now windblown,
Within the salt spray of the afternoon.
Rusting in the sounds of time,
in the negation of space,

Clues to inevitability,
brass ringed barriers padlocked,
Doors stuck in perpetuity amidst the cacophony of eons
Forgotten in decaying moments of ages spent
A key dropped in antiquity,
removed from memory.

A lost boy searching in the silicone
Sifting through the silence of generations
For that which had existed and must exist again
Looking for the key to the chains limiting the future
Finding only shells shattered by the surf,
Digging holes that fill with sea as they are dug.

A lost boy is questing in the dunes,
Delving in the sands,
sun bitten and burned,
Alone in the perception of a future
Lusting for freedom
to exit his cell,
to escape.

HE LIKED THE LOOK OF IT

Oh, he liked the look of it,
subtle in the morning light
Blue, and azure,
indigo,
royal purple,
grape or mulberry.
He saw it through the crack in time,
through the vacuum of thought
Reflected on the frieze above the windows,
through the stained glass partitions,
Panels of aquamarine and paisley,
strange in such a place,
But he knew he liked it.
It grew on you.

The lichen on the bricks,
green and silver,
reassured him
Of living things, living organisms,
even if they were leeches
Their task to suck life from the other.
He had tried not to be a sucker,
but you know what they say,
There's one born every day,
and he had been born in the day.

He had been born on a day with no one around,
not even a mother.

At least that's what they said, "poor boy, no mother"
No father either,
how could that be,
how was he conceived?
Did random sperm collide in the stratosphere with a lost egg,
Tossed aside in an arbitrary act of love,
and why do they call it love?
Had love been involved,
was he a love child after all?
He didn't think so,
but hell,
how can you tell in today's world?

He had missed that part of growing,
hearth and home,
a caring family.
He was sure he never felt loved,
never felt the warm moist teat on his cheek,
Except once in the dark,
in a corridor,
with a woman who wanted ten bucks,
Who showed him a nipple for suckling,
but he couldn't,

he didn't know why,
It just wasn't right,
somehow he just wasn't ready,
and renting it for a few minutes
was something he knew he just couldn't do.

But sitting in the cloister,
in the multi-hued light of morning,
it hadn't mattered.
He was content.
he was at ease.
He was ready for what was to come,
Though he had no idea what that might be.
Then out of the scarcity of morning,
the unprincipled light of morning,
The half-light of the day dawning,
his eyes seemed to lie,
to deceive,
For an apparition approached dressed in dread and relief.

He had been sleeping,
his spine pressed against the destruction of Jesus,
Protected from pagan spirits who could destroy him,
And the ray of sun had pried his eye to life,
to look,
and what did he see,

But that black robed phantom dressed in righteousness,
dressed in scripture,
Reaching to touch his soul,
if she could find it,
reaching to touch him.
With a start he woke full,
for why should she touch him,
he had been touched before.

"Stay away" in a voice sentient with fear and concern,
But it hadn't mattered,
those people never kept their distance,
Those people always did what they did,
when they did it.
She touched him
and he was touched,
touched to be touched,
in truth,
But it wasn't right, no matter,
for the touching took something from him
Took something that he wished hadn't been taken.

What she took wasn't coming back,
It was lost forever in the mists of light,
In the conflagrant web of sanctuary,
in the velvet cells of welcome.
Yet what she took, was but a piece of a whole,
minor but immense,
It was only a piece of skin,
only a pound of flesh,
no barely an ounce

But it was a piece of skin that could not be reconciled with belief
Only a piece of flesh,
taken,
not given,
ordained by those who ordain such things.

Did you know that flesh is flesh,
skin is skin,
gene is gene,
But only if you have the power to decide such things,
to determine?
The taking is the thing,
the bottom of things,
no more
no less
Yet the taking, the power, the control, the authority,
Is so overwhelming, so full of all that is,
how can one contend?
It is what it is and it is nothing more or less.

He sat,
the victim,
the saved,
the object,
in the light from above,
But the light was only the sun,
the morn,
as it rose each day, each year,
Though they taught it was the light of god,
the light of salvation.

He felt the warmth and it was not holy warmth,
not sublime,
It was the mundane touch of the day,
the daily cycle of creation that some
Attributed to a being beyond,
but when right,
was within the reach of each.

He aged with the teachings,
studied the writings to learn what was there,
He kept in touch,
he became practical in the extreme,
until he knew
the word was not his own.
He learned, became learned.
His skin gone,
his sacrifice completed in flesh and deed,
he found salvation in that moist teat offered for ten dollars,
in the pussy sold
without regard and without conscience,
to provide what is needed when it is needed.

What else is important in the world that exists,
in the world that experience dictates
But the sense that the skin tells all,
Offering of self to another is enough,
She had offered herself as a sacrifice,
as a playmate to those accepting,
A companion in the health of life,
in the psyche of the civilization.
What did she offer and when?
That is always the question,
for how else can society
prescribe blame, how
else can society deal
with that which is?
We cannot.

OPENING DAY

He glanced back across the intersection
over her head,
His hand still in hers, rushing
through the throng in the dusk,
Through the patrol cars and vendors of the intersection,
Burritos,
peanuts,
bottled water
and traffic control
The preposterous afternoon of spring and seed
The day park of the newborn,
through the April of the day,
To the wringing life of the day,
this start of the season.
Opening Day is no illusion,
no Midwestern fantasy of spring,
No grab of heart,
five fingered clutch of antiquity
But the source of hope,
the renewal of life,

In the red-seamed horsehide thrown at ninety plus,
She was with him,
sealed in the season,
locked upon his arm.
Her hand,
clutched in excitement, is real in this blue-skied orgy of light
This Woolworthian draw to the beginnings,
the origins,
She pulled him to the portal of baseball,
impatiently tugging
Toward the red bricked entry to the season,
Away from the superficial,
the business of business
Found the green diamond of release in the sun of the equinox
Opening Day,
the beginning,
the start,
where all are equal
Where each can be champion,
where all breathe life afresh,
Where all men are boys and all boys can be men.
Play Ball!

SHE STOLE HIS SHOES

She stole his shoes just before dawn
Cut the laces, eyelet by eyelet,
With her left-handed scissors
Worked her way through the left to the right
Then cut the toes out of his socks for good measure
She does not easily forgive or forget
After the fight, after her refusal to come to terms
And still, he stays with her.

She phoned every female friend he had
From high school through college to today
The weeks after their marriage
To announce the great news, the nuptials
Laughing a sweet hello to each
Through long distance and local
And still, he stays with her.

She was a refugee from religion,
Reveled in her revolution from the constraints
Leaped at experience and experimentation
Excited to know him, the instigator of different,
The creator of new, unique, and enticing
Until she was through, ready to return to religion
Ready to forgo the new, the exciting for the familiar
The retreat to the staid, and she did just that
And still, he stays with her

She finds fault with much that he does
Criticizes characteristics that drew her to him
Struggles in her connection to him
No recognition of the constancy in his beliefs
His bedrock of sustainability, his disregard for the preaching
That which she once found intoxicating, thrilling
She grudgingly connects, superficial inclination,
And announces she is pregnant
He will stay with her.

AMBER LIGHT

Saffron light dulcet through the filtering forsythia
Through the laced curtains drawn
indifferently against the night,
Through the morning that begins the day,
transforming eventide.
Emerging light gilds the walls,
the air,
our exhalations,
amber
Rounds shadows,
liquifies the edge of shade,
syrupy distortions,
Graces the sweet smooth skin of her back
uncovered during the sleep,
Her comforters strewn raffish, rumpled across her waist.

I reach a hand expectant,
To find her freckled frame,
my arm leaden in the gathering morn,
searching for her warmth,
to touch her solitude,
lost in sleep.
Divining the smoothness,
cool in the bronzed air,
stroke lightly
Down the muted ridges of her spine,
down the foothills of her frame
And round again, up and down the casualness of her reach
Caressing her fingers each in turn,
tracing her touch,
tracing her print.

Preceded by a murmur barely heard,
she rolls magically toward me,
Twisting her warmth into the crook of my arm,
settling into my embrace
Snuggling in the niche where she fits,
into the space promised to her for lifetimes.
My arm closes gently behind her, confirms her reservation.
Her hair rearranged,
falls careless on to my curled chest,
linked
intertwined futures.

I rest in the muted morning,
the light turning pale while shadows stiffen.
I am content with the morn whiling into day,
With the minutes morphing into hours
She is within my world at last.

IN A CELL COMPLETE

Amanda sat quietly, a lotus in repose,
Legs twined comfortably,
wrists lightly resting upon her knees.
Placid,
waiting for nothing,
caring for nothing,
Alone in the totality of life,
infinite deaths.
She was connected to the "it" and the "the"
She was all and none,
complete and empty,
She was a woman within the wisp of life.

Subconscious,
in the zone beneath and above the undivided
She had conquered barriers that shielded,
Stone caulked palisades,
leaching minerals into the soil
Decaying
and dissolving
within her creation.
She had never felt so alive,
so dead,
so anonymous,
so singular
In the search for the all knowing,

in the quest of the one,
The whole of the things set by time and zealous regard.

She settled amidst the stars shot like popcorn across the skies,
Watched the clouds of the day expand
and dissipate in instant charade,
Contemplated the flesh,
the bone,
melding with the all-seeing thing
that is and was and will be.

Becalmed in the glow of the "non"
the reality of the "un"
Amanda had become a soul diffused,
had become animus arrest.
She had become a ward of the state,
sweet in its care,
A protégé to be fed, and stroked,
in the isolation of her cell.

ONE WAY

There are two ways to go on a one-way road to nowhere
A dashed line inevitability toward the future or
The muted,
refusal to adhere, to resist
To take the tracks against the grain,
To travel in reverse dodging the pitfalls of previous lives
Oblivious to the swelling orchestral pronunciations of reality.

The soundtrack of the undetermined functional resurrection of self
Plays in the rounded,
pounded,
remaking of the soul.
The anvil and the fire crucial to the crucible of life
Within the stipulated reworking of the days
Slandered respites in the blood work,
broken bones and torn tendons
Taken in the minutes of rejuvenation
To create the signature,
the imprint,
the silhouette of nature.
The unborn charge into the void
Where the fringes of the accepted impede travel.

A lonesome track into the featured fury of the itinerary
Is the only way to manipulate that which can be changed.
Wrong-headed they charge
Wrong way they howl
when denying the policed instructions of life
Ignoring the directionals on the sides of the road
Finding truth in the orientation chosen,
in the refusal of safe,
Heading only to a future determined by the self,
Not the one-way visit to the ordinary
The dead end defeat of liberty.

MOON

Every time I look at the moon
It is somewhere else,
Not where it was before
Does that mean that the earth and the moon
Are circling in different orbits?
I want the moon to be where I can see it
When I want to see it.
Why is science so difficult?
Why can't I see the moon where I
Think it should be?
Reliant on my observations and wishes
Not tied to Newtonian notions of reality.
Today the half-moon sits in a sky-blue perch
In the middle of the day, but why?
It doesn't seem right, moons should show
Their structures at night, in the dark
Casting the sun's partnered light
Not, wasting their purpose in the afternoon
When the sun reigns supreme in light.
The moon confuses me and I don't like to be confused.

TEACUP OF TEARS

Their days were measured by tears in a teacup
But the teacup filled precipitously,
a teapot was required
And then a bucket,
a pail to collect the salty brine.
Their relationship was awash in tears,
too bad.
They shared a one-bedroom walk-up soaked in distress.
Tears had flowed
in torrents down the stairwell,
over the front stoop
across the avenue.
Drowning affection in the sewers below.
When at last they took breaths not saturated in regret
Their lungs filled with air
devoid of agitation,

When at last they looked through eyes dabbed dry
each was abandoned,
each was repulsed,
each was tainted.
The fabric of their conjoined existence had been rent
Depositing heartache in places foreign
without care.
The unreasoned choice of place and time was amiss.
Their memory filtered, mellowed through time
became elusive and vapid,
tears at least,
are real.
Tears had become covenant and security,
Had become the connection to another.
Intimacy
Tears had washed across their dependency in a binding
That when finally unstuck
shattered self.

I KNOW HOW TO DO THINGS

"I know how to do things"
he declared in a voice resonate with certitude,
But not from pride and self-importance,
not puffed with his own knowledge
It was an offer, nothing more.
And he did know,
if you wanted to listen.

But who listens today,
when the only voice that matters is the self,
The voice that can only be heard in mirrored rooms,
Where the visage reflected
is more important than the message
Where each and every,
ignorant and wise,
sound the same in echo.

"I know how to do things"
he said again to those who would listen
This time louder,
spoken to those in the back of the room
To those whose voices, sotto voce, are the voices heard
In the backs of rooms,
where the intellectual deaf gather.

"I know how to do things",
    he repeated once again, tenuously
He watched the wary eyes,
    the set of the jaws,
    the shoulders turned
It was clear no one really knows things,
    there is nothing that can be shared
He smiled benevolent,
    deflecting the corruption,
        tender.

"I know how to do things"
    he said, and he did.
        With a shrug,
        averted eyes,
            he withdrew slowly to the exit
    Head held high through the dispersing throng
        brushing shoulders,
            bumping ideologies
Collected his thoughts, his craft
    disappeared into the looming evening.

Today,
    knowledge is belief,
    belief is knowledge.
What is real,
    what is actual,
        what is truth,
            is what is believed
In the sanctuary of the self,
    in the sanctuary of churches,
Away from the constraints of intellectual inquiry.
    We are all the poorer.

HER VOICE

Her voice appeared
From the past still present
A recording of her laugh,
Voicemail,
once thought erased,
Sang in his ear.

He had erased the memory,
the message,
He was sure,
weeks ago,
a time when he still knew her.
A time when she was real,
A time when her murmurs had thrilled him.

Now in the seconds after the last minute,
In the days beyond the last life,
In the life behind his experiences,
Her voice came to him from the void,
Came to him from the electromagnetic ether.

She sounded...
She was real,
as real as he knew her to be
She sounded in his depths,
A siren's song of laughter,
on his recording,
In this life,
this memory,
this moment's space.

Her voice,
her enchanted articulation,
Was a trill of allure from another world
An echo of a time that was,
A reverberation of happiness,
Now only frustration
lost intent.

He had longed to remember that voice,
Remember the timbre
the tenor of its chords,
Ached to imprint its pattern on his cells
And knowing the importance,
the import,
He struck 'erase' again,
firmly,
she was gone
finally.

THE RIGHT WORDS

He has worried about the right words,
chosen carefully,
How to enunciate the factors crucial for so long now
But it turns out the words left after the onslaught
Were enough,
words said during the confrontation had no effect
Words thought so important in the moment didn't matter
When they gained no purchase,
no understanding
Only the words sighed in regret seemed to work
Through the phalanx of accusations and recriminations.
"I am sorry" was powerful, even when there was nothing
To be sorry about.
She hears through muffled responses,
she hears not.
Her righteousness regarding who she is,
is legendary

She cannot be mistaken,
she cannot be wrong
And he can only admit that he is the problem
to salve her feelings
To reestablish an ability to communicate.
He works at creating a sense of feeling,
of not being wronged by the unfair accusations
In the ritualistic dampening of emotion
But the last words,
The words of truth,
of concern
Are buried in the excesses of her denial.
What can he do?
What can he say?
Only goodbye

ILLUSION

Hector awoke on a Wednesday morn, and discovered
    he was still alive.
At least it appeared so. Everything seemed the same,
    Yet vaguely different, strange in some way not described.
The ochre walls, the green and tan coverlet,
    the blinds drawn against the night,
        All the same, all the norm,
        all the evidence that his life continued,
    But intuition warned of a change in degree,
        a precognition of a tidal shift, not forewarned.

An ambiguity existed that might signal an ending,
    and was that ending his?
He reached to the cool sheets beside his nakedness and
    she was gone,
        No sign of existence,
        no depression in the sheets, or wrinkle
        no warmth remaining from her body,
Only the cool void,
    smooth,
        implacable, lacking definition.

She had been there once, he knew it was true,
    and now she was not there.
Was he dead after all,
    and death was no more than the continuation of the death
Before he was dead,
    the lifeless score of his existence?
How can one tell if one is dead or alive, wanted, or maybe not?
What if he had been dead for eons and illusion was life,
    life illusion?
How could he be sure?
But wait,
    What if he wasn't dead, but she was,
        dead to him.
Is that why she was gone,
    is that why she left no tracer to follow?
If she was dead,
    she wouldn't be in his bed,
        she wouldn't be in this life,
            And she wasn't there.

She wasn't where she was, where he remembered her,
It made no sense, but all the sense in the world.
He knew it must be real,
He concluded dourly, he was alone,
Again.
With a squeak, a squeal,
the door to the bedroom opened haltingly.
There she was,
backlit amidst the chaos of morning,
Cups of steeped green tea in her hands,
nipples erect in the chilled air,
Her puff of black hair a magnet for his desires
Shining on milken skin that was unblemished
By life and presumably death.
She was exquisite in the day's new light.
He must be alive he decided.
He smiled.
She must be alive as well.
He was not alone on this morn's rebirth.
He came erect to accept the tea
affable amidst the pillows and expectations.
He was gleeful he was alive, could sense his toes and fingers.
Or, if this was illusion,
It was ok with him.

HUGS

A good night's kiss,
beneath a yellowed front porch light
chaste but heavenly,
lips caressing gently in the night
when I lied.
You
eyes widening pulled away
buried your face in my chest
hugged me
and said hugs were better.
I,
fool that I was,
and am
agreed,
nodded above your perfumed hair
and lied that a hug was enough,
hugs were better,
hugs were sufficient.

The kiss
exquisite beyond thought and anticipation,
rattled through my tendrils to the tips.
I would have given weeks or months to be with you,
to taste you to excess
but this night was over, the moment gone.
Alone on the curb
watching the stars circle Polaris
I wondered,
Did you feel it,
or did you bid me
leave
to save me the embarrassment?

SCRAPBOOK

She had a scrapbook of his future
An album of his life
Polaroids in black and white
Milestones he would achieve
And she showed him
Explained each story, photograph
She showed him the sun and the moon
The years into tomorrow
And he listened

She showed him her intent,
A desire to sculpt the potential,
The stone she had purchased on their wedding day.
She began with a fervor, knowing the future she had forecast
Knowing the dwindling days before failure.
Working with hammer and chisel chipping then pasting
In broad strokes, creating the template,
Plenty of time to polish and refine as time goes along.

He, trying to please, to fulfill her dreams
Settled into the daily directives willingly for a time.
Attempted to fulfill her predilections
To become the person she thought she had married.
That person who she could be proud to produce,
Proud to have holding her hand, smiling countenance
A monkey on a chain, dancing to her organ grinder rhythms.

The show promised by time and her promised resolve
Became a calamity of false pretenses and affectation.

Who shall decide the fate of the future, the form of the art
Decide the paths that will be taken but the self
The travails of the growth of the person developed in congruence
With perseverance and intuited understanding of the self.
He is a man, distinct in his body and soul,
Determined to decide his future, not prescribed by another.
He might be what she wishes, but on his terms, not hers.

DREAMS

Dreams are messages from the deep
Subterranean calls from the ether,
the unknown known
Preaching sermons from the soul that are hidden
From conscious regard,
noted awareness
Speaking in languages not studied.
An interpreter is required who speaks dreams
Who can decipher the meaning of pictures in the night
or sunlit moments of excruciating reality
That reveal the nature of the beast to be released,
And what is that beast, what will it look like?
It is constant that there is movement, growth or
Deterioration that will occur,
never stasis
Never the ever foretelling of emotion.
They say you will explode into the inner you
The you that satisfies reality.
What does it look like?
What is the chance?
Who is the inner you that will be exposed?
What if you don't like that inner you?

MONDAY

ALICE

Loam,
Bacterial,
Anaerobic humus
Beneath fingernails and reputation
Grounded firmly and rooted, Alice moved.
She charged,
Dragging great clods of clay and stone
Bumping down the meadow's path
Creating a Hansel and Gretel trail of naivete
Alice moved with a purpose
She moved with a porpoise to guide
Her windward path, beating down the wind
Dancing with sea urchin toes, beneath
Constellations of starfish fixed with rubies
And crawling in the morning,

Yawning
from beneath a mollusk bed
Stretched her willowy wings, waxing in the waning wind
She grew,
Composted, flowered and matured.
Fruit flowing from her cells floating on the wind
Amidst the petals of spring for all to taste
For all to smell
Welling bursts of welcome for strangers and friends
Alice says well come,
And stay
Until you can stay no more or less
Tend your gardens liberally,
Spread mulch in spade fulls
Grow your tomatoes and corn
Cultivate and propagate,
Yes,
savor,
The herb and spice and weed.
Alice loves you,
None the less.

ON FRIDAY NIGHTS

On Friday nights beneath October moons
on browning fields under klieg lights
I dressed in epaulets and turquoise, silver braid
ramrod straight,
lips pursed,
poised for 15 or 20 minutes of action.
My father loved me, and mom,
But no shouts of "Down in front" so they could see unimpeded.
There was no fatherly braggadocio
that his son
played trumpet in the band,
marched between the hash marks
was merely a link for our heroes,
between the halves,
filled the void between tackles and blocks.
They twisted and moved, caught views,
not quite sure
without names across our backs, or numbers,
which of the trumpets I was.
They said they saw me,
were proud,
It was nice of them to say so.

I marched and played
songs that few wanted to hear.
Now the dance squad,

the cute skirts hiked about their waists,
Pubescent legs long and thin
drew the boys' attention,
The grass stained, muddied heroes drew the girls
But the band,
well the band played and marched,
formations built on trust,
announced and reinforced with imagination
for no one was high enough
no Goodyear blimp to see what they formed,
only the amalgam of bodies side by side,
strutting, stopping, playing,
erect in the dirt
then scurrying to the side as the heroes ran between us
ran through our lines
delicately weaving through our predetermined path.
We disappeared into the dark and the arena
roared to life once again.
As the heroes struggled, scored, and were scored upon,
My life took different tacks,
away from the lights and the whistles.
I spent the second half scoring in the bus with Janet,
Who played the flute and had wonderful lips.
She played my instrument behind the drums,
in the back of the bus.
While the heroes struggled mightily in combat serene,
And the crowd roared or groaned,
I in the back of the bus
Groaned and roared as Janet played me in expert tones.
I've always liked football.

WHEN THE BOY WAS SEVEN

The class moved to the music portion of the day
Recorders
each had paid one dollar
except
The second-grade boy in the first seat in row two
He hadn't had the one dollar when it was due.
The teacher to occupy his time
gave him a book to read at the edge of the class
A book he would read seven times
and then stare at the pictures waiting
To return to his place in the class
While most students were taught to toot on their recorders
The boy was taught as well
He was taught the lesson of poor
A lesson he would never forget
The knowledge that poor is a condition over which he had no control
At the age of seven

Poor is poor they say, not as smart, or competent.
Look at him sitting on the edge of learning.
Why don't his parents take care of him?
Doomed to follow in the family's footsteps
Too bad little boy at seven
you are consigned to the poor
Those left behind.
This little boy,
who was a learner,
began to learn new lessons
He was a learner of all things,
and will continue to learn
What will he do when he is ten or twenty,
or when he reaches his awareness
The boy of seven will attack the norms
As he grows, matures
Will stare down the naysayers with withering eyes
Will grow into that which they could not foresee.
He will attain and succeed
And never sit at the side of the room again.
He will always know the meaning of poor,
Always know the sense of poor,
But he will prevail
In the chase for the future.
Poor is a state of mind now rejected

SERPENTINE TONGUE

Monday morning shadows slide
Across the spread
Morning moves inexorably toward day
And I, covers tucked about my neck
Like puckered lips
Watch three-piece suits and spiked heels
Grow from the far side of Market St.
Inclined upon my billowed Babylonian throne
Surrounded by all and nothing
I am a thief of the day
As I steal and file the visage of normality
The sights of society, still born
Buried deep beneath sheets and comforters
Coverlets and fear, I grow
Shedding obscene and foolish self-perception
Like a rattler's skin
My biologic cocoon feeds life and soon
Flashing serpentine tongue and
Peacock's tail, I will fly
Or perhaps, bee.

UNDER A STAR

That boy was born under the Star of David,
Or was it the Lone Star of Texas
Or could it be the Star of the Nazarene?
Oh fuck, at least there was a star
On the night he was born,
that blazed bright
His mother had said he was special.

He was special, he was one of a kind.
He knew it growing older
He knew it each night when the skies darkened
Each night, when the stars blinked on
Each night, when the sun blinked off in global descent.
Each night in the musk centered smoothness within his hand.

In darkness he stood astride the earth in certitude
Locked on the north star,
Exigent memories
Of a glittering light at birth
that would guide him in his works
Beneath the milky skies of the northern hemisphere
Beneath the sparkling milky way,
He was whole and he was everything that could be.
The night was his and his alone.

Half a life would be enough he swore in solitude
The remainder, the day, was unimportant.
The deprivations of a life without light were nothing.
He was special; he had been born under a star of destiny,
He knew it was clear, was infallible.
His mother had said it, she could not be wrong.

As he grew within the aura of his mother,
The light grew inside him,
No other was required.
It was the illumination of his power and control
Dominant he knew,
Complete if he wished,
Unrivaled if he decided
Hidden to all except his mother,
His creator.

Within the nuclear reactions of home and hearth,
    Within the settling arms of the woman, the womb
    The boy settled in comfortable self-absorption
Knowing the extraordinary,
    His gift,
        Would be obvious to one and all
            In time.
He had been born under a star of repute,
    A star of significance,
        Whatever the hell that star might have been.
His mother had told him so.

SCHOOL EULOGY

Frog seeing eyes
Stare through cinder block walls
At ponds full of trout and tadpoles
Ignoring the square root of 2

Frog seeing eyes extending through glass panes
Reaching for cloud rolling skies
Without verb centered sentences

Pine thought mind in unencumbered flight
Through limitless mirrors and windows
Oblivious to Robert's Rules of Order

Pine thought mind
Invincible, faster than can be fathomed
Cannot be contained in six sided centers of learning

Freedom

LIGHT ON THE CORNER

Night slips through the branches
At the edge of the yard
Crawls between the slats of fences
Fertilizing the mysteries and fantasies
Of Young Boy between the sheets

The light on the corner was broken long ago
The city hasn't fixed it

Young Boy, a good boy, was responsible
In before the witching hour
Compliant and obedient
Never disgraced a mother or father
Who were always proud.

The street light on the corner is broken
The city should fix it.

Young Boy, yes sirred and no sirred
His path through childhood
Shook hands with a firm grip
Looked people in the eye
When he spoke when spoken too

The street light on the corner will not be fixed
It shines darkness about it.

Young Boy could be trusted, told secrets
Of friends and people he knew
A depository of whispers and fears
Backseat embraces, lips slushed one against the other
Hands grabbing flesh and fur

The streetlight on the corner stays broken,
Young Boy needs it fixed
Young Boy was responsible...
Yes Young Boy is responsible and he knows it

Momma's love and Daddy's too was immense
He felt that love
Press on his chest
Constrict his throat
And suck the light from his eyes

Young Boy knew he was loved because he was good
And getting better beneath the broken street light

Eliminating flaws and faults
Ridding self of imperfections
A boy to be proud of
A boy to keep within their love
A boy that sang the party line
A boy growing into boyhood

The streetlight remains broken and Young Boy
Sits closely in the dark it casts
Where only he is aware

Imperfect limbs, incomplete conscience
Tears and fears, withered smiles
And empty eyes.

Young boy has learned to love the streetlight dark
He hopes the city has forgotten
To look
To see
To repair

Young Boy wears satin shirts and wool
Owns contact lenses and tortoise frames
He combs his hair
Once, and only once a day
And Young Boy has a smile or a wink for all
Facades of friendship
Young Boy has a heart that only he will see
Buried beneath his bones

Young Boy recollects, revives the streetlight
Broken on the corner
And mulls what he might do

The city has forgotten
They won't fix it
It's no longer theirs
The problem of solving its darkness is denied.
It is a happy thought.

PATTERNS IRREVERSIBLE

In patterns irreversible, down one-way escapes
In paths that cannot be traced
We move through portals, tunnels, streets
Through alleys damp with night
We move in random lefts and rights
In dizzying u-turn spins undeterred in half light
Down narrow cracks in skyscraped walls
Asphalt patched and quiet
We move among the many, the throngs
Between headlight shining walls
That reflect, deflect, and confuse in troubled wrong way turns
And each must follow one-way streets without recourse
that have been laid before with no retreat
One-way streets that lead to further one-way streets and more
No retracing decisions, or redoing that which we did
It is done in the moment often with little regard
There are signposts if we watch, but why look when there are
Red lights, green lights, stop signs, yield
For god's sake yield.
We move in forsaken spaces where the sun will never reach
Blackened bases where flowers dare not grow.
We are children, childless, in the groaning future.

WHAT A BOY

What a boy he was
Searching for that which could be
Open to the promise of the future
Naïve beyond repair, beyond his knowledge
The echoes of a past without guidance
Without direction or purpose
And yet he persevered, groping through
The labyrinth of society,
The tangle of obstacles and roadblocks
Society has erected to maintain the status quo.
He is an interloper,
Not quite accepted,
Yet he is hard to ignore,
A budding threat to those in control
Of the levers of society,
the ladders of success.
Some are frustrated by their inability to control this boy,
A few feed his future with thoughts of success,
Feed his quest to achieve and master the systemic malaise.

What a boy he was,
What a man he will become that some
Will emulate and model
And others will be appalled by his progress.
He stands astride the circumference,
Not quite in
But does his best to distort the dimensions,
Does his best to challenge Pi,
to increase the area allowed.
He is a challenge and a challenger
And he will not stop.

A GOOD NIGHT

Her breasts pushed full against the silk and lace restraints,
puffing extremities
creating a chasm of enticement
Desirous of his touch
Yet bashful in the light of the night,
And he,
a gentlemen of sorts,
did not reach,
did not touch,
For the skin soft blush of her bosom was not offered.
She leaned toward him in the front seat of the car
Leaned to give a little good-bye kiss
Accentuating the promiscuous display.
He kept his eyes up
on her face
Leaned to accept the kiss.
He noticed she closed her eyes as their lips met
He watched her take the few steps to her door,
She stepped inside,
waved and disappeared
It had been a good night
And maybe they will have another

POCKET OF AIR

It was as if he was trapped alone,
Sunken in the hold of the carrier
tethered to a relationship that was under water
Committed to the ongoing pretense of caring,
Straining to keep nostrils above the floe,
the flood of emotions,
constrictions,
debilitating deflations.
Resting upon the ocean's floor within the cocoon of oxygen
created by the daily regimen.
A slim pocket of air below the ceiling,
sucking life from
The decreasing margin of sustainability
Nose pressed to the ceiling,
Little time left for recrimination or denial
Writhing for existence in a world
Of senseless vacillation
Wondering if salvation was possible
If it could be saved.
When she offered a lifeline, a contract
A lifesaver to grab, but only if he agreed
And finding the terms unacceptable
Decided to let it die.

CRACK IN THE WINDSHIELD

There's a crack in my windshield
A pebble thrown on the highway of life's destiny
Growing and twisting each day,
each turn a stroke of art
For it has been revealed.

That fissure is not just a crack,
a message has been sent to me.
It's an epistle from beyond for those who can see
It was no accident,
no mistake,
no, it can't be ignored
That crack is a silhouette of Jesus.
It's true by God.
Praise the lord,
hallelujah,
the message is:
I'm rich, I'm going to be rich.

They'll all want to see it,
mothers and sinners, but
Greedy I won't be,
no, greed is a sin
It'll only be a dollar,
no maybe two,
no three
To see the silhouette of Jesus
Sculpted on the windshield of my Jeep.

It's a holy vision,
a creation of God
That crack in the glass,
the window of awe
And the IRS can't touch me,
it's religious you see,
A shrine,
a church,
a place to meditate and ponder
How rich that crack is going to make me

DREAMS OF PASSION

In dreams of passionate complexion,
unfocused,
through lenses belied
We kissed,
long and slow,
endlessly
on the lips,
stunningly voltaic,
breath taking
sensations essential,
So real in my sleep that my soul stood attention,
Rapt in the sensuous touch
of memories unbidden.

In dreams
I cuddled you,
Arms wrapped round
Reliving warmth wrapped in afghan,
the enchantments of sin forgiven,
And waking,
staggered by the intensity of senses
arrived in the dark plastered world of my life,
The bedroom,
the house,
the screened, gated windows
impinging my survival.

Blinking wide,
startled to consciousness,
It was a dream and nothing more in this existence,
A piper's cloud of invocation and prayer.
The shadowed existence of certainty,
a poor silhouette of the truth,
in mournful obsidian.

NOBODY DID IT

He didn't
She didn't
They didn't
But somebody did.
It was done before dawn,
Done before the rooster's crow
Accessing the last minute before
The glorious rebirth of the day.
He said it wasn't me
She said it wasn't me
They said it wasn't them
Yet it was done.
There is no denying that it was done
But who did it?
It's hard to say.
We know someone did it.
But who?

NO OUTLET

The sign said NO OUTLET
Black letters on a yellow diamond
Attached to a post in the road.
I looked and thought
If I can't let it out here, where can I?
What if I need to let it out,
Is it against the law to let it out here?
Is there a sign somewhere
Black letters on a yellow diamond
That reads LET IT OUT HERE?
A place to let it all out,
I don't think so,
but if you see one will you let me know?
And STOP
All capital letters on a red octagon
Commanding obedience
When we all know it is difficult to
Stop on command
I have tried numerous times
Almost always unsuccessful
Tried with all my might.
When is STOP the best path,
When moving on may be better
May help us conquer that which haunts us
Dealing with that which is, rather than
STOP.

Then there is YIELD
A triangle on a post less intrusive
More friendly it seems, more like a request
A conversation even
Yet still it wants us to give in
Not stand tall for what we believe
There are times to yield I suppose
Times to take the alternative route
But YIELD neglects the alternative
The desire to take a stand against
Stupidity and negativity
Whatever the odds.
Why aren't there signs
That deny the prohibitions
That are designed to guide our tethered future
Signs designed to help and succor?
Why not signs that say
GO FOR IT or
YOU ARE CORRECT or
RIGHT ON or
YES?
Signs of affirmation that would
Help us to succeed
Heaven knows we could use them

PLAY GROUNDS

New playgrounds for play neon and chrome
Searching for playmates to share the dare
Finding Jungle Jims and Mary-go-rounds
Making the rounds unchaperoned, pretentiously
Striving for hot tenor sax in smoke filled rooms
The wail of the sirens of jazz and jiz
Caught between screen and self
A choking deep in the throat
That croaks I love you
In 15 different languages

Playgrounds for play none of them staid
Catnip and speeding through cloverleafs of love
Through turnstiles at the A and P
Searching for lettuce, discovering cabbage
Questing for princes and princesses
To supplement the playground toys we know
Populated with all manner of soul
Filthy little beasts all around the grounds
Cooing as they defecate on the general
Marble silent in victory and reward
Marble solid in the soiled air
Shitting in 15 different languages

Playgrounds for play childhood lost
Silent but for the memory of life
Giggling wickedly in our ears
Where no other sound exists
We swing, a treasure chest of touching, teetering
Suspended above the gravel lined floor
Avoiding the hurts and pains of scraped
Elbows and knees and conscience
Suspended on chains of steel, fastenings secure
Cold links between our fingers, taut in the day
Soaring over treetops and clouds
Afraid to let go, to fly in the face of gravity
We hold on to our safety, white knuckled
Hold on to the anger and feel the fear
Of 15 different languages

Yesterday before the moon had filled
And tides crashed high on New Jersey shores
Children played in playgrounds secure, guarded
No eye contact or smiles amid reckless nights
We were those children who disappeared
Buried beneath aluminum slides, hot on a summer's day
Amid treasures of rock and bottle tops and gum
Monuments erected in 15 different languages.

THE SON RAGING ROSE

The son raging rose,
driving the ragged moon to oblivion
Startling the night into rainbow array,
Creating a day
A day of sensuous splendor,
moist and gratifying
A day of champagne and sugar fresh from the cane
Creating a space and a time that she filled.

She
with the down soft skin of tremulous touches
She
with the melodic laughter of Homeric legend
She
with the robes of lavender wrapped round her
Drank black tea from
a coppered cup,
colored mocha with cream
She
Spread apricot jam on toast in languid strokes.

The son raging rose,
bravely,
audacious,
reckless in his quest,
Suffered from the assault,
wounded in thought,
word
and deed,
Agonized and was beaten back in misery
Falling silently to despair
and darkness once more,
And she
her fingers buttered from the bread,
Became ashes and bitterness,
melancholy
and sorrow.
The son sank,
hissing his disease into the sea.

SHE WAITED

When last she saw him,
He said he would call
So she waited.

Sunrises melted into sunsets of a thousand days
Moons waxed and waned in numberless succession
And she waited.

Rivers swelled with rain, spilled from their banks
Withered and dried from drought
And she waited.

Mountains exploded, eroded, disintegrated
Silting deltas, remolding the land
And she waited.

Ten million breaths, ten billion heartbeats
Neurons by the trillion aligned to remember
While she waited.

She would wait
Because
He said he would call.

NATE

Less than a handful
Of arms and legs
Trying to grab a hold
In this new world
My son

Fighting demons and dragons
In great grunting breaths
Sucking life
Into his spidery frame
My son

Confronting the end
Before the beginning has begun
With a smile that could thaw the Saturnine wastes
And bloom daffodils through the January freeze
My son

Scrawny, fragile conqueror
Winner of countless struggles
Your name is Jonathan
You are Nate
My son

STARS

It is dark, night has fallen
Where are the stars?
I sit waiting for the onset of stars
I need to see stars, to connect to the cosmos
There is ambient light filtering from the city
Creating a color that disguises the sky
I need to find dark skies
To see the Milky Way.
The city as most things shadows reality
The real, the intense is muted to survive
We drive to the mountains
To Marble, to the back country
To witness the billion star panoply of
Our Milky Way
A view beyond expectations
Beyond what we could dream.
Sitting in a spa on the outskirts of reality
We are awestruck at the immensity
Of stars and sky
Our wish at that moment
That all could witness this display

SUNDAY

SUNDAY

I've been listening to music, all genres
Reading poetry by the bushel
I have arrived at the conclusion
That everything has been said
Every emotion has been examined
From every point of view.
Maybe nothing more can be added.
It's Sunday, we all need to reset
Good wishes to all
On Sunday we all need to rest.
We can start again on Monday.
Let's rest today.

ACKNOWLEDGMENTS

Waynelle Wilder who helped me relearn the ability to dream

My supportive and talented family
Nate and Misty
Jay and Jennifer
Blake
Kate

My friendly critics and readers
Marcia Goldin
Mike Agee
Mary Sornsin
Terra Monson
Irene Griego
Tom Crabb
Bonnie Gertz
Candice Ferguson
Marisol Jurado
Steve Berger
Lindsey Kline
Cynthia Stevenson

Kirsten Jensen-Shepard

Bobby Haas-Editor

Victoria Wolf-Graphics and Format

Kelly Weaver-Photo

My favorite inspirational teachers
Mrs. O'Connor
Mrs. Hallbeck
Miss Lynen
Mr. Ellis

And finally, the Spirits swirling in my dreams

ABOUT THE AUTHOR

REARED WITH THREE SISTERS, married for the first time at 19, then married to his second wife for 47 years plus three years of "living in sin," coupled with working in a profession that is predominately female (public education) means John has indeed "Lived With Women" his entire life. He was the first in his family to attend college, earning a BA and an MA from Northern Colorado and a JD from Denver University. When he started his law degree his mother said, "Don't you have enough degrees already?" He smiled and said, "One more." He was a passionate middle school teacher, principal, and central administrator for 48 years, earning his law degree while teaching. When he finally retired, he accelerated his interests as a gardener and learned to use the bounty to become a skilled cook, especially the varied cuisines of Italy. John enjoys good food and fine wines, has traveled extensively, both internationally and domestically, and has focused on his golf travels, eventually playing golf in all 50 states. He is thrilled by live theatre and exhibits a life-long enthusiasm for performance. John is currently fascinated by the aging process, the ongoing march toward obsolescence in mind and body, and the struggle to stay physical and alert. He is currently living alone in downtown Littleton, Colorado where he has cultivated relationships that he maintains regularly. He dreams daily and continues to put one foot in front of the other.

Visit johnpeeryauthor.com for New Work

www.ingramcontent.com/pod-product-compliance
Lightning Source LLC
LaVergne TN
LVHW100522110826
845146LV00002B/745

* 9 7 9 8 9 8 7 8 8 4 5 0 8 *